RAISING
CHILDREN
WHO SOAR

A Guide
to Healthy
Risk-Taking
in an
Uncertain
World

RAISING CHILDREN WHO SOAR

A Guide to Healthy Risk-Taking in an Uncertain World

SUSAN DAVIS, Ph.D.

NANCY EPPLER-WOLFF, Ph.D.

Foreword by Jonathan Cohen, Ph.D.

TEACHERS COLLEGE PRESS

Teachers College
Columbia University
New York and London

Published by Teachers College Press, 1234 Amsterdam Avenue, New York, NY 10027

Library of Congress Cataloging-in-Publication Data
Davis, Susan (Susan Elysa)
  Raising children who soar : a guide to healthy risk-taking in an uncertain world / Susan Davis, Nancy Eppler-Wolff ; foreword by Jonathan Cohen.
    p. cm.
  Includes bibliographical references and index.
  ISBN 978-0-8077-4997-5 (pbk.)—ISBN 978-0-8077-4998-2 (hbk.)
  1. Risk-taking (Psychology) in children. 2. Child rearing. 3. Parent and child.
  4. Parenting. I. Eppler-Wolff, Nancy Jo. II. Title.
  BF723.R57D34 2009
  649'.6—dc22

                                                                      2009012956

ISBN 978-0-8077-4997-5 (paper)
ISBN 978-0-8077-4998-2 (hardcover)

Printed on acid-free paper
Manufactured in the United States of America

16 15 14 13 12 11 10 09   8 7 6 5 4 3 2 1

To my husband, John, and my children, Jacob, Sarah, and Matt
–NE-W

To my daughters, Emma and Abigail
–SD

And to our parents, Heinz and Ruthe, and Lowell and Barbara

CONTENTS

Foreword *by Jonathan Cohen, Ph.D.*   ix

Acknowledgments   xi

Authors' Notes   xiii

Introduction   1

Redefining Risk   2
Our Risky World   5
Parenting for Good Risk-Taking   6
The Connection Between Parent and Child:
   Temperament and Risk-Taking   10
What About Risk-Taking in School?   11
Raising Ethical and Moral Children: Risk-Taking and Tolerance   11
Putting It All Together   12

1.   What Is Risk?   14

Our Definition of Risk-Taking   15
The Changing Definition of Risk in Society   19
Four Qualities of a Good Risk-Taker   23
Introduction of Our Parent-Child Pairs   27
Learning the Power of Risk: Beginning a Risk Journal   31
Pragmatic Steps Toward Thoughtful Risk-Taking   32
Summing Up   35

2.   Child Development and Risk-Taking   36

Overview of Child Development   38
The Importance of Understanding Development   43
What Are Universal Emotional Risks?   44
How Risk-Taking Unfolds With Development   51

Learning Style and Risk-Taking   55
More of Life's Bumps and Risk-Taking:
   Divorce, Illness, and Loss   59

3. The Parent's Part:
    Self-Reflection and the Practice of Listening   **61**

The Process of Self-Reflection   62
The Practice of Listening   72

4. The Parent-Child Connection and the Threads of Risk   **86**

Temperament and Risk-Taking   87
The Parent-Child Fit and Risk   92
How This All Begins: Understanding Attachment and Risk   96
Attachment and Risk Beyond Infancy   97
The Neurobiology of Risk   101
How Does This All Come Together?   103

5. Risk-Taking in School   **108**

The Foundation of Learning   109
Temperament, Learning Style, and Risk-Taking in School   114
A Guide For Developing Good Risk-Takers in School   121

6. Risk-Taking, Independent Thinking,
    and Tolerance Toward Others   **127**

Risk-Taking and the Peer Group   128
Risk-Taking and Breaking Barriers   132
Service Learning Programs for Young Children   137
Scientific Explanation for Taking the Risk to Care   143
Compassion Is a Learned Behavior   144

7. Putting It All Together:
    Parent-Child Activities for Good Risk-Taking   **146**

Games and Activities to Encourage Risk-Taking   147
Doing Community Service as a Family Activity   163
Putting It All Together   164

Suggested Readings   **167**

References   **175**

Index   **183**

About the Authors   **193**

FOREWORD

Life is dangerous. Parents know this. One of the wrenching aspects of being a parent is that we learn over time that we can never fully protect our children from the dangers and problems that inevitably scare and scar them.

This wise and practically helpful book redefines risk. Risk is usually understood as referring to the chance that something will go wrong. But, Susan Davies and Nancy Eppler-Wolff suggest that there are both good risks and dangerous risks in life. They suggest that dangerous risks represent moments when children impulsively jump into the unknown. Good risks are moments when children reflectively consider the unknown: "Does this feel right and make sense to me?" "Is this something that I want to do now? And if so, what are the range of ways that I might do this now?"

In fact, risks are a foundation for learning. More often than not, if we are totally comfortable with a situation, new learning seldom occurs. And at the other end of the spectrum, if we are filled with fear, there is little or no learning. It is when we are feeling some anxiety, some uncertainly, and some sense of risk that extraordinary discovery and learning can occur.

This volume is a sophisticated yet practical guide for parents that supports mothers, fathers, and guardians helping children in learning to take wise risks. The authors not only understand child development, but are able to translate research from developmentally informed neurobiology and psychology and social, emotional, and ethical learning into very practical frameworks and suggestions.

This book, however, is not just about theory. It is sprinkled with a series of short narratives about children's experience at home, in the playground and at school in ways that make the ideas and suggestions come alive. There are many wonderful and practically helpful suggestions. For example, the authors wisely focus on promoting children's self-reflective capacities. In many ways, being reflective provides an essential foundation for almost all forms of learning. Just think about the moment when you encounter a new problem or decision. Whether this is a new mathematical problem ("When have I seen problems like this in the past?") or a social decision ("Do I want to do this with him or her?") reflection provides an essential foundation for learning. "How do I feel about this?" "If I am not sure what to do, who can I turn to for help?" "What does this problem or decision remind me of?" These are just a few examples of self-reflective questions and considerations that help us to be wise risk-takers as opposed to impulsive ones. But the authors of this book go much further. They present a developmentally informed framework to help parents think about what different kinds of risks mean to children of ages 3 to 10. They present a series of concrete, practical steps and strategies that provide helpful questions, frameworks, and suggestions for both parents and teachers.

Additionally, this book also helps us to listen more deeply to our children. Listening provides such an extraordinary foundation for learning and being connected to our children.

Over the last two decades, a growing body of research has shown that social, emotional, and civic learning provides an essential foundation for children's healthy development. Parents are always teaching children "lessons" about risk-taking, listening, and reflection. Sometimes we are conscious and intentional about the social, emotional, and civic lessons we are teaching; too often we are not. This is a book filled with wise counsel, thoughtful and practical guidelines, and resources for parents and educators that support teaching our children the skills, knowledge, and dispositions that provide the foundation for success in school and life.

—*Jonathan Cohen, Ph.D.*
President, Center for Social and Emotional Education

ACKNOWLEDGMENTS

Almost 3 years ago, when we began the first draft of this book, we wanted to share our ideas of risk-taking and development that grew from our professional practice as psychologists, our experience as teachers, and our role as mothers. At the genesis of this project, though, we were unaware of another equally important source of inspiration, our friendship. This book is a result of that deeply respectful and joint creative venture.

We thank Meg Lemke, our editor at Teachers College Press, for seeing the potential in our work. Meg, thanks for taking a risk with us, and for shepherding this manuscript through the editorial maze. We also thank the rest of the team at Teachers College Press.

So many of our friends and family encouraged us during the long gestation of this manuscript, but one friend, Esther Fein, saw the promise of this work from the very beginning. Esther, thank you for your love, astute insights, and capable editing.

Our collaboration at the Learning Center of the Jewish Board of Family and Children's Services (JBFCS), which took place over 10 years ago, marked the beginning of our friendship and professional partnership. We are grateful to Dr. Marsha Winokur, our friend and mentor who passed away during the summer of 2007, for seeing the possibilities in our collaboration and in the programs we created at JBFCS and for supporting our efforts to take smart risks as we created and developed the mentoring programs at JBFCS.

We also thank Resa Eppler, Judith Greenberg, Anna Ruth Henrigues, Nancy Crown, Carol Colman, and Marcia Colvin for their encouragement, constructive comments, and careful readings at various stages of the manuscript.

Our assistants—Sara Zoeterman, Jake Wolff, Sarah Eppler-Wolff, and Nicole Best—spent many hours checking references, editing, formatting tables, and generally helping us get the manuscript into good form. We thank you all.

Thanks go to Dr. Adam Davis and Dr. Michael Golub, our neuroscience consultants, who provided invaluable edits in the section of the neurobiology of risk.

We also thank our photographers, Matthew Wolff and Alex Remnick, who so ably captured the spirit of parents and children taking risks together! And to our models—the Nickman family; Judith Greenberg and her son Sasha; Soraya Gomez-Crawford and her two daughters, Isabella and Alexandra; Rafael Fernandez and his children, Kiara and Kyle; and Esther Fein and her daughter Natasha—thanks for your patience, generosity, and beauty.

We thank our mothers, Barbara Davis and Ruthe Eppler, for letting us know how proud you are of us and for reading our draft manuscript while carefully keeping the loose pages in precise order. We know that we can always count on your love and support of our work.

Finally, we thank our families, who lived with us, inspired us, and encouraged us from start to finish:

John, I know that I can count on you in ways too numerous to list; I love you. And to my children, Jake, Sarah, and Matt, thank you for your constant love, and for being patient during those many, many hours when I was "on the computer in my office."—*Nancy*

Thank you to my children, Emma and Abby, who inspire me to be the best parent I can be. You also show me in so many ways how my hard work and passion in writing this book filled you both with pride and inspiration to follow your own passions. I love you both beyond the universe and back.—*Susan*

AUTHORS' NOTES

Risk Is Gender-Free

The integration of good risk-taking into our lives is a universal phenomenon and not gender specific. Our model of good risk-taking applies equally for girls and boys, and men and women. Therefore, throughout this book, rather than using cumbersome gender-free language, we randomly alternate between using male and female pronouns.

About the People We Describe

The parents and the children we describe throughout our book are fictionalized composites of people we have known from our clinical practices and personal lives. We have disguised and changed individual characteristics to maintain confidentiality.

INTRODUCTION

During the first period of a man's life, the greatest danger is not to take the risk.

—*Sören Kierkegaard*

This is a book about risk-taking. Risk makes us feel alive and helps us grow. It teaches us about fear and courage. Yet risk-taking can also be dangerous.

This is a book written by two psychologists who are also parents. Over the years, we've seen hundreds of children and parents in private practice, schools, and community centers. This is a book that encourages each of us to look at the relationship between ourselves and our children—so we will be better equipped to launch confident, respectful, productive children into the world. In this book, we introduce a novel concept into the field of child development and parenting—namely, risk-taking—and we assert that it has an essential place in raising our children. Without the challenge of risk, there is little growth; and without growth, development falters. Therefore, raising good risk-takers is essential. The focus of this book is on teaching parents the value of good risks, and how to teach their children to take risks wisely and freely. Being a parent is one of life's most complicated yet deeply rewarding endeavors, and this book educates and enriches this process.

This is a book that teaches our readers how to impart the skills of good risk-taking to their children and students. We know that learning is an active process. Our preschoolers, who learn about the world through block play or dramatic play, know this. Our grade school children, who study medieval history through creating their own pageants and murals about the subject, know this. Educators and philosophers have told us that we learn through doing. Yet, as adults, we sometimes forget this. We invite our readers to take a risk to engage actively with this book. Read. Mull. Muse. Write notes in the margins, and begin your own journals. Send us your comments online (www.raisingchildrenwhosoar.com).

We begin with some questions. Why can one child take personal risks necessary to propel her toward life's achievements, such as trying out for a gymnastics team or venturing into a new friendship, while another takes impulsive and dangerous risks such as skateboarding in traffic? Why does one child embrace the challenge of working hard and tenaciously toward his goal, while another shies away from any challenge that can bring potential failure? What is our role, as parents, in this process? Aren't some of our children more prone toward risk-taking than others? What do we do when our child continually takes bad risks? One parent told us, "When I go to the playground with Kyley, I just hold my breath and hope that we won't end up in the emergency room. That girl scares me!"

REDEFINING RISK

What is risk-taking? And why is it a key concept for parents to understand? In this book we focus on emotional risks—the everyday chal-

lenges that put our children on the precipice between success and failure and that require them to take a leap into the unknown. A child's
risk-taking style is a product of her innate temperamental makeup, the
ongoing parent-child relationship, educational experiences, community values, and other life encounters. In this book we trace the stages
of positive risk-taking over the course of a child's development. We
integrate current research and practice and illustrate how risk-taking
changes as a child grows. We focus on the ages between 3 and 10, a
crucial time of development for the child in which the foundation for
adolescence and adulthood is created.

In this book we teach parents how to raise good emotional risk-
takers: individuals who can leap at life's opportunities and tolerate
the inevitable shortfalls that happen along the way. In Chapter 1 we
introduce and describe various ways sociologists, psychologists, and
other parenting experts have defined the concept of *risk*. Risk has pri-
marily referred to the dangerous elements of contemporary culture, so
parents naturally have thought of it as something to avoid.

The Upside of Risk

In this book we redefine risk as positive. We explain that risk not
only has its upside, but also that it is unavoidable; and it is through
everyday experiences with risk that our children learn the pleasure
of success, and the coping skills to weather the frustration of failure
and persevere. Failure, in and of itself, is not the antithesis of good
risk-taking. Instead, it is an important component of it. Children need
to experience failure to know that it won't destroy them and that they
can bounce back from it. If we don't—or can't—allow children to
make their own mistakes, to work through uncomfortable feelings,
and to experience disappointments, then we are limiting their development.

Good risk-taking can also foster feelings of self-confidence and competence. Over a half century ago Eric Erikson (1950), the renowned developmental psychologist and psychoanalyst, discussed not only the
importance of risk-taking, but how it is tied into development:

> The strength acquired at any stage is tested by the necessity to transcend
> it in such a way that the individual can take chances in the next stage
> with what was most vulnerably precious in the previous one. (p. 263)

Erikson understood that as a child masters the skills integral to a particular stage of development, he will later use these achievements to take risks necessary to meet the challenges of the next stage. As parents, it is one of our central responsibilities to encourage our children to meet everyday challenges. Good risk-takers also tend to be more resilient and motivated children. This book teaches parents the concrete and pragmatic steps in risk-taking so that they can, in turn, teach them to their children.

In Chapter 1 we also introduce four prototypical parent-child pairs who are working together toward good risk-taking. These duos are fictional composites of parents and children we have known over the years in our clinical practices and personal lives. We hope that you will see elements of your families reflected in these stories, and that you can learn from them as you embark on your own risk-taking journey.

Meet Katie and Dylan

One of the parent-child pairs is Dylan and his mother, Katie. Dylan is a shy child who began speaking his first words at the age of 3. As a young child, he would carefully observe others, often relying on family members to speak up for him. At home, his family appreciated his quiet style—his clever wit and his sensitivity—and would instinctively give him as much time as he needed to express his thoughts. They helped Dylan focus on his strengths, not his weaknesses.

Katie, who had grown up in a family that was wary of risk-taking, worked on her own self-reflection. She understood how important it was to neither patronize nor be critical of Dylan's difficulties. Katie worked with Dylan's teachers to reinforce the support he received at home. Although Dylan had some teachers who were too quick to judge him as being less able than he was, Katie advocated for her son to help teachers understand him and his learning style. Often, as we will see as Dylan's story unfolds in this book, teachers were able to support his risk-taking in the classroom, and, at other times, they were not. Luckily for Dylan, he had more good school experiences than bad ones. Overall, he had a strong enough foundation during the important formative years for him to develop a good risk-taking style despite his vulnerabilities.

In late elementary school Dylan had a teacher who valued and encouraged his written expression. Before long, Dylan became interested in journalism and in middle school began writing for the school newspaper. When he was asked to become editor-in-chief of the school newspaper in high school, he hesitated, thinking, "How can I be the head of the newspaper when just talking to people sometimes still makes me so nervous? And, what if I stammer?"

Despite these doubts, Dylan took the risk because of the confidence he had developed. At the end of his senior year, his school newspaper won a national award for excellence. He had also earned the respect of his staff and made some lifelong friends in the process.

Did Dylan experience some anxiety, fear, and self-doubts when he considered and then accepted the job as editor? Did he take some bad risks along the way? Yes, he did. But a culmination of years of taking smaller risks and experiencing both successes *and* failures taught him the value of taking the next step. Dylan is an example of a child who successfully, though not easily, learned to take on life-enhancing risks throughout his childhood.

The Downside of Risk

At times we have all taken bad risks. In third grade a very frustrated Dylan lied to his teacher about having lost his math assignment when in fact he had torn it up in anger. As he impulsively tore up the paper to avoid feelings of vulnerability associated with getting a poor grade on the assignment, he was taking a poor risk.

A bad risk emerges impulsively, and it is often self-destructive. Poor risk-taking often surfaces from a lack of confidence or poor self-esteem. The class clown is an example of poor risk-taking emanating from low self-esteem. This child has come to feel bad about his academic abilities or social skills and resorts to being a nuisance, albeit a funny one, to get attention.

OUR RISKY WORLD

Many parents share concern that our world today is far riskier than when they were children. There are stressors that range from personal to global. On the individual level, many children experience intense academic and social pressures. Additionally, there are a range of outside threats that parents and children face. There is, for example, the possibility of terrorism that even young children are aware of as they travel in airports, train stations, and bus terminals with their parents. Preschoolers feel the profound effect of intensive security screening. And even young children can't escape the pervasive messages of danger in our media-saturated world.

It is sometimes hard for parents to know how to proceed. On one hand, we want to encourage our children toward achievement and success; we nudge them to get "out there" and compete (Anderegg, 2003; Elkind, 1988). Many parents feel a responsibility to prepare their child for our competitive global society. At the same time, many parents feel a strong need to protect their children in an increasingly dangerous world. One parent said, "Between screening my daughter's television watching and prohibiting various computer games and Internet activities, I feel like instead of the FCC I'm the 'HCC,' the 'Home Commission on Censorship.'"

All of this affects our children's risk-taking. Some children who are pressured to succeed will naturally rise to the challenge and generally take good risks toward achievement and mastery. But some children will recoil from the challenge, and perhaps, like the class clown described above, turn to bad risk-taking behaviors.

Likewise, some children will approach risk-taking with relative ease. Other children, perhaps those who are more porous, will respond to the fear that they hear expressed through the media, parents, and teachers, and will either stop taking good risks or turn to poor risk-taking in a mistaken effort toward self-protection.

So, what can we do to mollify these pressures? How can we raise our children to become thoughtful, confident, and productive adults when there is great societal pressure to push them to succeed, and to shelter them simultaneously? How do we prepare them to take smart risks when present-day life can be a breeding ground for bad risk-taking?

PARENTING FOR GOOD RISK-TAKING

There are four components of parenting toward good risk-taking: understanding the development of risk-taking, developing a practice of self-reflection, developing a practice of listening, and understanding how the parent-child connection impacts risk-taking. Through learning about these ideas and through practicing these strategies, parents can raise children who are good risk-takers—children who can soar.

Risk-Taking Is a Part of Development

In Chapter 2, we introduce our readers to the idea that risk-taking follows a predictable developmental sequence. At different stages, our children want and need to venture past their last achievement and into new, unfamiliar territory. The specific "developmental tasks" of each stage correspond to our children's needs for safety and growth, and there are common risks associated with each stage.

In Chapter 2 we also discuss six universal risks that we take throughout life and describe the emotional states that are often associated with taking these risks. In this chapter we also introduce how we can influence our children's risk-taking style, and we discuss individual differences in risk-taking style.

MEET CHARLES AND TIFFANY

Charles and his shy 2-year-old daughter, Tiffany, are another of our parent-child duos. Charles is an outgoing, social man. Since birth, Tiffany, by contrast, has reacted to new experiences in a fearful, anxious manner. Unlike other children at the playground who squeal with pleasure on the slide, Tiffany is frightened, not only of climbing on the monkey bars and going up in the air on the seesaw, but also by the other toddlers who are impatient to have a turn and threaten her physical and emotional space. This is especially painful for Charles who would so dearly like to see his daughter playing happily with the other children.

In this brief anecdote we see that for Tiffany, a shy child, learning to climb while socializing with friends is a particularly difficult risk. This story continues later, and we learn how Charles helps to temper Tiffany's fears.

The Practice of Self-Reflection

Parents who practice self-reflection and careful listening are prepared to guide their children toward developing a good risk-taking style. In Chapter 3 we teach parents how to develop these important skills.

Through self-reflection we understand how our own risk-taking style affects our child's and how it was shaped by temperament and childhood factors. This process is important in helping us assess our impact on our child and in overcoming our own fears—fears that can interfere with our child's ability to take sound risks.

In Chapter 3 we will detail the process of self-reflection so parents can understand the ways that—deliberately and unwittingly—we influence our children's development.

The Practice of Listening

The third component toward raising good risk-takers is honing the ability to listen to our children. Parents who have done the work of self-reflection are ready to begin the practice of listening that helps us to distinguish between what our *children* need and want and what *we* need and want.

While it may seem that we are listening all the time, most of us are not very good at really hearing what our children are communicating to us. Learning to listen well, like self-reflection, requires careful practice. It also facilitates a strong parent-child bond—something that is well worth the effort. Listening well also helps us understand who our children are temperamentally, and where they are at developmentally. In essence, listening helps us develop a sixth sense as parents— the uncanny ability to *know* our children. This process strengthens the parent-child relationship while it fosters good risk-taking across development.

This is similar to the ability a parent of an infant has to hear the difference between a cry of hunger and a cry of physical pain. As a child grows, we take these skills further. For example, when a 6-year-old screams, "I hate you, Daddy," after a family fight, the parent needs to ascertain what his child is really saying. This can be a difficult task! The child's outburst could indicate a number of underlying feelings. For example, is the child feeling frightened that you will relinquish your love and affection toward her? Is she unable to contain her feelings of frustration because you were unable to contain yours? Is she being rude and/or manipulative? When we develop the self-awareness that comes from self-understanding and learn to listen well, we also develop greater emotional flexibility and an enlarged perspective. This enables us to simultaneously better realize our own strengths and weaknesses—taking our narcissistic needs out of the equation—and also better know what our child is trying to say to us so we can respond appropriately.

MORE ABOUT CHARLES AND TIFFANY

Charles had been practicing the skills of self-reflection and listening and began to put them to use one Saturday morning when he took Tiffany to the playground. It was early in the day, and there were no other children nearby. Charles thought that this would be a good time to encourage Tiffany to practice her skills on the slide. After a number of attempts, Tiffany was happily going up and down the slide—until another child approached her. Tiffany was at the top of the ladder when another child climbed up rapidly behind her. Tiffany shouted, "No! [Get] down!" She shoved the boy away. The other child's mother was irate. "Your daughter shouldn't shove! You need to teach her how to share!"

Charles, who was at once embarrassed and surprised, was primed to react with anger toward Tiffany. He realized though, through his own self-reflection and by listening and observing carefully, she had achieved much that morning. He knew that a reaction of anger would undermine her progress. Yet he knew that it was important for Tiffany not to shove other children, even if she was feeling uncomfortable. Quietly and calmly he explained to the mother that Tiffany was frightened and that, indeed, he doesn't tolerate pushing or shoving. (Unfortunately, the mother wasn't feeling very warm toward Charles or Tiffany and walked away angrily after saying, "Just keep your kid away from mine!")

Charles was now upset and wanted to lash out at the mother. He took a couple of deep breaths instead, and met Tiffany at the bottom of the slide and took her to a quiet part of the playground. There he explained that even if she is feeling scared she is not allowed to push other children. He emphasized how important it is to use words, not pushes, to convey feelings.

"Why did that lady scream at us?" asked Tiffany.
"Because she was feeling angry, and she was using her words with us."
"That makes me mad!" said Tiffany.
"I feel mad too, Tiffany, and that lady should have used nicer words toward us, but you can't push or hit other children. You

need to *talk* to them instead. But I want to tell you that I am proud of you for going down that slide this morning. It was fun, wasn't it?"

Here Charles was teaching Tiffany the rudiments of positive risk-taking on the playground. He was saying something like, "Go for it on the slide even if you are scared" or "Use your words to express your fear as opposed to physical violence." He was teaching her how to tolerate strong and uncomfortable feelings. It might have been easier for Charles to blame the other mother instead of looking at his own contribution, but he knew that he too had to manage these feelings.

THE CONNECTION BETWEEN PARENT AND CHILD: TEMPERAMENT AND RISK-TAKING

In Chapter 4 we delve deeply into the ways that the parent-child connection affects your child's risk development. This is a mutual process; parent and child each affect the other in a myriad of individual and idiosyncratic ways. And there is not a certain style, relationship, or trait that necessarily predicts good or poor risk-taking.

In Chapter 4 we explain how temperament affects risk-taking. We link the concept of temperament to the propensity—or difficulty—one has in taking all sorts of risks. Some children are spontaneous and natural risk-takers and others need to be taught how to take risks. We know that some of our children are shy and prefer to be alone. Others are fiery and excitable; still others are slow to react. These and other temperamental attributes affect risk-taking.

Yet this is not quite so simple. We show that the parent-child relationship mixed with the child's life experiences powerfully impact on the development of the child's temperament, and thereby his risk-taking style. While temperament is genetically based, current neurodevelopmental research shows that temperament is more malleable than once thought (e.g., see Kagen, 2006). We have all heard friends or acquaintances say, "I used to be such a shy kid. Now I am not the least bit shy."

The bold and brash toddler may or may not take the best risks as he develops. Nor does the highly anxious mother necessarily limit her child's good risk-taking. In fact, the parenting tapestry is rich and complicated and can entail twists and turns as the development of both parent and child proceeds. We maintain that by understanding these separate and interweaving factors we can become wiser and more skilled parents, and thus we will be able to teach our children to take the kinds of risks they need in order to soar in life.

WHAT ABOUT RISK-TAKING IN SCHOOL?

Parents who understand the importance of nurturing good risk-taking with children at home, can witness the powerful effects of their work. Our children tend to be motivated for achievement and also resilient to withstand inevitable disappointments and failures. But what about risk-taking in school? What happens when our children leave home every day? Can risk-taking be integrated into the school curriculum? How can parents and teachers partner on this effort?

Your child's school experiences contribute to her risk-taking development just as your child's temperamental tendencies and home learning environment set the stage for how she will approach risks outside the home. In Chapter 5 we discuss the templates for learning in school, namely, the balance of security and risk that allows for optimal play and work. We follow the course of risk-taking in school, and we address how the child's temperament, the child's learning style, and the collaboration between parents and teachers influence risk-taking in school. We develop a guide for parents and teachers to work on thoughtful risk-taking development.

RAISING ETHICAL AND MORAL CHILDREN: RISK-TAKING AND TOLERANCE

In Chapter 6 we discuss the relationship between risk-taking and tolerance toward others, particularly those who are dissimilar from us. One of the fundamental goals of parenting is raising ethical and moral children who can contribute actively and thoughtfully to their communities and to society.

For many, the ability to think independently, or "out of the box," entails taking definite risks. How do our communities and the schools that we send our children to affect this process? For example, what if we are living in a mostly ethnically homogenous community and send our child to a school with little diversity? Or what if we are living in a homogenous community but our child attends a racially diverse school? How do we react when we hear one of our children's friends utter a racial slur? What if we grew up in a family that thought of a particular nationality, race, or religion as inferior or bad? How do we dare to question long-standing moral or social norms? What do we do when our own child is the one who is disrespectful toward another religious or ethnic group?

Daring to challenge our own or others' established beliefs takes a certain confidence, strength, and ability to think for ourselves. This entails risk. Questioning what we were taught to believe or what others around us believe can shake up our sense of identity and put us in conflict with those with whom we're close.

Tolerance for others—for an individual or a group—and thoughtful questioning of values yields growth and understanding. This learning starts when our children are young and continues through life. Having the skills to take good risks in response to preconceived notions and prejudices takes the concept of risk-taking to a larger scale. In Chapter 6 we enlarge the issue of risk-taking further and discuss pragmatic ways for parents to teach their children to engage in risk-taking as it applies to values and beliefs as well as social and political action. We develop a model service-learning plan that parents can create for their own children.

PUTTING IT ALL TOGETHER

In Chapter 7 we provide a series of parent-child activities that promote thoughtful risk-taking behaviors. These activities have been developed through our experience in our professional practices working with parents and children and with our own children. These activities help families embrace a philosophy of healthy risk-taking together. We also urge parents and children to have fun and to be creative when playing these games.

Healthy risk-taking facilitates self-confidence, fosters an ability to work and play with all kinds of people, and allows children to venture forward in life. The venerable Dr. Seuss playfully captured the essence of good risk-taking in his book, *Oh! The Places You'll Go* (1990). His proclamation to children also speaks to parents as he writes about the challenges of risk:

> When things start to happen,
> Don't worry. Don't stew.
> Just go right along
> You'll start happening too . . .
> KIDS, YOU'LL MOVE MOUNTAINS!
>
> You're off to Great Places!
> Today is your day.
> Your mountain is waiting.
> So . . . get on your way!

Chapter 1

What Is Risk?

The purpose of life is to live it, to taste experience to the utmost, to reach out eagerly and without fear for newer and richer experience.

—*Eleanor Roosevelt*

Risk. Danger. Threat. Peril. For most of us—especially parents—risks are cliffs to avoid. Small risks are minor hazards; large risks are perilous ones. So, shouldn't we steer clear of risks for ourselves, and for our children, whenever possible? Why should we learn about supporting our children's risk-taking?

The answer is that parents have a fundamental responsibility for understanding the inevitability of risk: It is a fact of our existence. As children grow, they become more and more independent, and they will encounter risk every day of their lives. Risk-taking is essential to child development and is a vital part of parenting. Through teaching, nurturing, and practicing good risk-taking skills, children will be better prepared to meet the challenges of everyday life. In this book we create a tapestry of risk that is interwoven in the context of family, school, and community. It is a tapestry because the way risk-taking unfolds in human development is anything but linear—it is a multilayered, multidetermined process. We explain how we can help children understand, approach, cope with, and master risk—each an integral part of their growth and development in an uncertain world. Through the development of thoughtful risk-taking, our children will be better equipped to leap at life's opportunities and rebound from life's disappointments.

OUR DEFINITION OF RISK-TAKING

We begin with a general definition of *risk-taking* that grows from the writings of a number of thinkers on this subject, including Denney, (2006), Lyng (2005), Hyland (1984), and Smith (1998). These sociologists and anthropologists are not well known to most parents. Their theories, however, are pertinent for understanding the importance of risk—both the upside and the downside. These researchers generally define *risk-taking* as a leap into the unknown. Most of their research focuses on the deleterious effects of poor risk-taking for adults or teenagers, including the use of recreational drugs or unsafe sex. While their research is an important foundation for our understanding of risk, in this book we focus on emotional risks faced by younger children: the risk to leave Mommy at the day care doorway, the risk to sing a solo in the school chorus, or the risk to persist in learning mathematics when the concepts are extremely challenging. We focus on thoughtful—or good—risk-taking, which we define as the ability to make the everyday decisions and choices that involve a conscious leap of thought, feeling, or action. When young children practice good risk-taking, they are not leaping into the unknown, but building a bridge to avoid possibly devastating risks later on.

While the risk-taker is striving toward growth, there is also the possibility of failure. As discussed in the introduction of this book, failure, in and of itself, is not the antithesis of good risk-taking, but just one component of it. In contrast, impulsive—or bad—risk-taking is behavior that emerges without judicious and careful thought, feeling, or action. It is a leap that may have self-destructive elements whose primary impetus is not toward productive growth. Impulsive risk-taking often emerges from a lack of confidence and self-esteem. Examples of poor risk-taking would be a 10-year-old boy who takes his friend's dare and walks on an active train track, or an 8-year-old girl who wants so badly to be cool like her older brother that she ends up skateboarding in traffic. What about the 11-year-old girl who struggles with academics in school, but makes the choice to not study for a test? She's avoiding trying to learn the material because she feels inadequate, and in this case, not taking action becomes an action in itself, and is a risk.

We all take—and avoid—good and bad risks from the time we can crawl. When a baby first gets up on all fours and takes his first movement forward, he is taking a risk. Many risk-taking behaviors, like crawling, unfold predictably with development. Some do not. It is important for parents to understand that there are different ways in which we, and our children, approach or avoid these risks. The ways in which we come to approach risk are influenced by six major components:

1. The parent-child connection
2. The temperamental styles of both parent and child
3. The child's age and stage of development
4. The parent's background and approach to parenting
5. The influences of school and community
6. Life's lumps and bumps (e.g., serious illness or loss)

Throughout this book we explain how these factors interact with, and impact upon risk-taking style, and we help parents decipher the extensive research and literature from the fields of psychology and psychotherapy, child-development, and neuroscience.

A Brief Introduction: The Components of Emotional Risk

We begin with a fundamental principle: Risk-taking develops largely in the context of the parent-child relationship; a child's risk-taking style emerges through the ongoing give and take interactions between parent and child. There is no particular type of child or a particular type of parent-child match (e.g., shy parent with outgoing child) that bodes well—or poorly—for the development of good risk-taking. In fact, all children can become good risk takers, no matter how they are wired, or what happens as they grow. This finding is consistent with contemporary neuroscience research that indicates that the human brain is far more flexible than people thought 20 years ago. (See detailed discussion in Chapter 4.) Psychologist Daniel Goleman's books on emotional and social intelligence (Goleman, 1995; 2006) teach us about the reciprocal effects of human brain development and the powerful role of environmental learning. His groundbreaking synthesis of concepts have contributed to a shift of focus in psychology, education, and parenting, and have made us aware of the central importance of emotional intelligence (a set of traits or skills, not measurable through standard IQ tests, that allow us to understand and manage our emotions and navigate relationships adeptly and wisely). The development of positive emotional risk-taking is a facet of emotional intelligence and its development contributes toward emotional competence.

Furthermore, temperamental traits that used to be considered static and unchangeable, such as shyness, are now found to be more fluid (Kagen, 2006; Kagen & Snidman, 2004). As a child's brain and temperamental style develops, her risk-taking style can also shift and change. Parents have much power to guide and influence children's risk-taking style to allow them to thrive in this complicated world. For example, the child who might be hesitant to take the motor risks (learning to walk, jump, or skip) that first emerge in toddlerhood may find the risks in the preschool stage less challenging and more natural. In Chapter 2, we discuss the developmental trajectory of risk in detail.

Our own risk-taking styles, which are comprised of our temperamental styles, our life experience, and our approach to parenting, influence the development of our chid's risk-taking. For example, a job promotion may have an impact on a parent in a number of ways, and her worries and concerns, as well as her excitement and joy, are all conveyed to her child and affect how he approaches risks. Again, this is not a simple process. It is not that natural, universal parental concerns will transform our children into poor risk-takers, or vice versa. It is that we, as parents, must come to understand ourselves well enough to know how our behaviors and feelings are affecting our children and how we can consciously modify these dynamics if necessary.

Our child's experiences in school and community also impact upon her risk-taking style. For example, if a family makes a move to a new community just as the child begins first grade, the child not only reacts to the inevitable changes of a move, but she is also affected by the subtle (or not so subtle) changes in the values, philosophy, and tenor of the school and community. Some schools, either because of their philosophy or methods of teaching, can inadvertently thwart children's attempts to take good risks. A school whose philosophy rewards correct answers and minimizes the importance of the process that goes into learning can dissuade children from taking intellectual risks. For too long, intellectual and social-emotional learning were regarded as separate entities. Psychologist Jonathan Cohen (1999) initiated a collaborative effort to study social-emotional learning and to create curricula that incorporate it into academic lessons, and broader school experience. Educators around the country are now implementing these programs in schools. Cohen and his colleagues have found that incorporating social-emotional learning into the school increases self-esteem and academic and interpersonal success. The development of positive emotional risk-taking is a vital part of social-emotional learning.

Communities that place great value on conforming to external norms and expectations can, over time, hamper an individual's ability to take personal risks. This doesn't mean that a child who attends this type of school or lines in such a community is destined to become a poor or avoidant risk-taker. In fact, there are many opportunities for parents to help their children become good risk-takers even in schools and communities in which risk-taking is not encouraged. In this book we provide our readers with the information they need to foster good risk-taking for their children. We help parents and teachers understand what the underlying sources of risk-taking are and how they can impact upon their children's risk-taking style.

So, What Is an Emotional Risk?

An emotional risk, like a physical risk, is a leap into the unknown. This leap places the child on the narrow, and often frightening, precipice between success and failure. While some research has categorized individuals in terms of their risk-taking, our clinical practice indicates that there are as many types of risk-takers as there are people; we each have a unique fingerprint for risk-taking. A risk for one child may not be a risk for another. And, while all risks represent a challenge of some kind, not all challenges are risky.

Let's go back to the illustration of Charles and Tiffany from the introduction. For Tiffany, both climbing on the monkey bars and tolerating her peers' impatience on the playground are risks for her. That vignette shows that Tiffany was moving beyond her comfort zone as she felt the uncertainty of whether or not she could successfully climb and also tolerate another child encroaching on her space. For another child, like the boy whom Tiffany shouted at and shoved, climbing the ladder may be a challenge, but not a risk. He was not, at that moment, standing at the frightening edge of success and failure.

THE CHANGING DEFINITION OF RISK IN SOCIETY

To fully explain the importance of risk-taking for our children, we take a brief detour into the history of risk and how this concept has evolved over time. Most historians trace the development of the term *risk* to the medieval period during which this word was used in regard to maritime insurance. With the development of a shipping industry to support rapid exploration, certain "risks" were calculated to understand the probability of possible dangers that lurked in the unknown sea journey ahead (Giddens, 1991). *Risk* was a term used specifically by the maritime business; the population at large had little use for the concept since most people believed that danger—or risk—was the will of God. Natural disasters, such as widespread disease, devastating storms, or famine, were thought to be under God's control. This way of thinking changed dramatically with the emergence of industrialism and the subsequent modernization of society in the eighteenth century.

How We Became a Risk Society

Urlich Beck is a German sociologist who has written extensively about how we have become, in his words, a "risk society." He explains that the widespread cultural and social changes that took place beginning in the eighteenth century significantly changed the ways in which we view risk. The Industrial Revolution brought private industry and urbanization to the masses, and these changes in living and working conditions impacted the way people thought, socialized, and lived.

With the rise of industrialism came the rise of individualism. People came to believe that their decisions could influence their fates. They became concerned about the probabilities—the chances—of danger in work and play (Lupton, 1999; Tullock & Lupton, 2003).

The twentieth century brought an influx of all sorts of risks. The inherent risks in nuclear weapons, for example, gave rise to what Beck calls a "risk society" (Beck & Willms, 2004). According to Beck, in modern and postmodern society there is an implicit tension between societal advancement and risk. The very advances that were supposed to enhance our lives have in fact jeopardized our health and well-being. In very recent times the advancements of images and messages of the media, Internet, and global communication are largely positive, yet our young children are sometimes exposed to too much information.

Individual Differences in Risk-Taking

There are also a number of experts, mostly sociologists and anthropologists, who have studied the development of individual differences of risk-taking style from a cultural perspective. Mary Douglas (1992), for example, writes that the ways in which individuals respond to societal expectations influences their risk-taking development. She has found that people who tend to conform closely to societal expectations tend to take fewer risks than individuals who believe that their fate is due to chance or luck. While these findings are important for parents because they identify some important individual risk-taking differences, these experts focus almost exclusively on the cultural components of the development of risk-taking. We have found that while the cultural factors of risk-taking development are vital, there has been little attention paid to the equally essential psychological and interpersonal aspects of risk-taking development.

Are *Edgeworkers* Good Risk-Takers?

Stephen Lyng, a sociologist who also studies risk on an individual level, explores the positive potential of risk-taking behavior, focusing on people who take part in potentially dangerous hobbies (such as mountain climbers) or careers (such as astronauts). To refer to these people who work and play on the boundary of safety and danger he coined the term *edgeworker* (Lyng, 2005). This novel and nicely descriptive term aptly captures the vitality of risk-taking. Lyng asserts that individuals who engage in edgework do not find risk-taking to be dangerous because they believe that their individual expertise will prevail over danger (cited in Cockerham, 2006). Lyng notes that edgeworkers gain great satisfaction from their achievements, and through the knowledge gained from their specific skill sets, they not only avoid situations that are overly dangerous but they also continue to reach greater heights, personal satisfaction, and growth as they take on greater challenges.

The concept of edgework risk-taking is intriguing for parents who are learning about the trajectory of their child's risk-taking development. Parents want to know why some children are more prone to risk-taking and also what contributes to the development of a good— or poor—risk-taking style. As parents, we ask ourselves: Is it in our children's best interests to teach them to become edgeworkers? Another sociologist, William Cockerham (2006), describes the psyche of an edgeworker in greater detail:

> Edgeworkers are not typically interested in mere thrill seeking or gambling because they dislike being in threatening circumstances they cannot control. . . . Thus, they do not like to leave their well-being to others or to the whims of fate. What edgeworkers seek is a chance to use their skill in dealing with a challenge, not turning their fate over to someone else. . . . Their own personal competence is what they want to put at risk, so they can draw on their own performance to construct an image of themselves as members of an elite. (p. 12)

This description of an edgeworker describes risk-takers as high-level achievers who are in pursuit of controlling the unpredictability of their world. The notion of being an edgeworker may not be appealing to many of us. Most of us are not wired—or emotionally made—to be comfortable with extreme risk-taking. It is uncomfortable to ponder teaching our children to live on the precipice between danger and safety. It is hard to believe that there can be much benefit to this way of thinking.

Yet we believe that in the context of the parent-child relationship it is possible that each of us can achieve the benefits of thoughtful— and safe—emotional risk-taking. When good risk-taking becomes the norm within a healthy relationship, trust and comfort with risk develops from infancy. Children who have a healthy risk-taking style tend to thrive on their achievements and better tolerate their failures. Good risk-takers generally have less to prove to others and gain satisfaction and confidence from their actions.

What We Can Learn About Risk from the Playground

Smith (1998), an educator who looks at children's risk-taking from observing children on the playground, makes a number of interesting contributions to the study of risk-taking. Smith describes the differences between high-stakes risks, and the everyday risks that we all take. Everyday risks are the risks of speaking up in a group, even if you are feeling shy, or initiating a new friendship, even if you are not naturally outgoing. This is a helpful distinction; yet as parents, we know that a 4-year-old can find the potential failure associated with a challenging game almost as daunting as jumping from an airplane. To young children, small risks can feel big and serious.

Risk requires that we experience uncertainty. We are required to do more than that which feels comfortable. We must dig deep within ourselves and test the limits of our abilities and resources. Taking a risk is the project of "encountering the unknown" (Hyland, 1984, p. 130). Encountering the unknown, experiencing uncertainty stretches us toward new self-understanding because we are enlarging our concept of ourselves and what we are capable of.

Through the observation of many children on the playground we learn that risk-taking is a skill that needs to be nurtured and taught, and this often requires the help of an adult, usually a teacher or parent. A child who is fearful of approaching the monkey bars would be taking a good risk by developing the confidence to start climbing. When the adult thoughtfully observes the child, he can guide the child toward good risk-taking.

What the History of Risk Teaches Parents: Where to Go from Here

Overall there is a notable lack of literature that studies thoughtful risk-taking as an important part of the development of young children. This is largely because most people, risk experts and laypeople alike, believe that the primary goal of the study of risk-taking is to predict, avoid, and control prevalent dangers in our contemporary world. Researchers examining risk tend to ask questions like, What are the risks of giving our children packaged baby foods? What are the risks of living in an apartment that was painted with lead paint? What are the risks associated with putting my 6-month-old in day care? Although these are excellent questions that need to be answered so that parents can sufficiently protect their children from harm, we need to focus equally on the upside of risk and how we can simultaneously help our children take on new challenges.

Experience and research has taught us that avoiding bad risks without learning how to take good risks is shortsighted for our children. The development of a thoughtful risk-taking style gives our children tools with which to prevail and soar in this risky world.

FOUR QUALITIES OF A GOOD RISK-TAKER

How can we recognize a child who is a thoughtful and smart risk-taker? She is generally a confident, happy child who takes pleasure from her achievements. She tends to feel strong and successful as she challenges herself to venture beyond her comfort zone. Being a good risk-taker, however, does not inoculate a child from the many vicissitudes of life. There are times that a child who has been raised to be a good risk-taker is anxious or unhappy, even for extended periods of time. She may experience difficulties in adjusting to a new school or developmental phase and may even make some relatively poor choices along the way. These periods of frustration and disappointment may be exceptionally hard for her—and for her parents to live through. Yet our years of observing children and their parents have confirmed that good risk-takers who experience a bump in the road tend to rebound well from life's scrapes and bruises.

For example, Jenny, whose family moved from a small town in Georgia to New York City, lost not only the home that she had lived in from birth, her school, and her friends, but also her beloved ballet. When she moved to New York, she wasn't sure whether to continue dancing. She felt overwhelmed and knew that the ballet world in New York City could be very competitive and rigid. Her mother understood Jenny's love of dance, so she wanted her to audition for high-powered classes immediately; but she also understood that Jenny needed to take her time in warming up to new situations. Jenny's mom, herself a go-getter who had high career status and had been valedictorian of her college class, did some self-reflection and realized that it was *her* need for Jenny to audition for these competitive classes, not Jenny's. After observing and listening to Jenny, she advised her to take some time to warm up to her new home and make new friends. Soon Jenny was ready to take the risk of enrolling in a dance class at their neighborhood community center. This was a measured risk for Jenny, one that she was prepared to take.

Figure 1.1 outlines four crucial qualities of a good risk-taker. These are universal attributes of good risk-takers across age and developmental stages. The examples we use to illustrate these concepts in this section represent a range of risks that commonly face the toddler and school-age child. (Chapter 2 discusses in more detail the risks intrinsic to each developmental stage.)

A GOOD RISK-TAKER GOES FOR IT—AFTER THOUGHTFUL CONTEMPLATION

First, in a thoughtful way, a good risk-taker "goes for it." What do we mean by this? We have found that successful people tend to reach just a little beyond where they are; they are able to take measured leaps to take on new challenges. They also know that there is a time and place for just "laying low" and going slow. Some of us do this rather naturally; others must develop this skill. Let's go back to the example of the toddler who is just learning to crawl. While learning to crawl is considered a usual part of the developmental progression for most children, we can observe a wide range of individual differences in how they get up and go. Some children just get up and scamper across the room. Others observe carefully, for a period of time, and then move ahead slowly and carefully. What varies from child to child is how they approach this developmental milestone. Neither of these styles is intrinsically good or bad, but the observing parent makes note of the ways in which her child approaches the risks inherent in early physical movement. Over time, parents learn how their children approach risk.

How can we encourage—or temper—risk-taking? We know that the child who is a careful observer as he learns to walk, will tend to exhibit this characteristic as he approaches other risks. Again, this is neither good nor bad. Rather, it is helpful information for parents who will learn how to enourage, or temper, their child's actions. For ex-

---

FIGURE 1.1. Characteristics of a Good Risk-Taker

- A good risk-taker goes for it—after thoughtful contemplation.
- A good risk-taker can tolerate disappointment and failure.
- A good risk-taker is tenacious.
- A good risk-taker takes pleasure and pride in her achievements.

---

ample, later on when this same child is learning to ride a two-wheeler, his cautious and careful nature may make him wary of approaching this challenge. If his parents know this about him, they can prepare him for the activity by first letting him observe others riding and familiarizing him with the mechanics of the bicycle. They will know not to rush the process. They can also make this experience even safer, and more gentle than usual by beginning the activity on soft grass rather than pavement.

A Good Risk-Taker Can Tolerate Disappointment and Failure

The second important characteristic of a good risk-taker is that he can tolerate disappointment and failure. In our clinical practices, we often hear parents tell us that they don't want their children to feel disappointed or to experience failures. They say, "I hate to see her so upset" or "I want her to have what I never had—security and self-esteem—so I want to be sure she always feels like she's winning." Children's failures and frustrations can be difficult for parents, since we all want our children to be happy. We have spoken to many teachers who are concerned that well-meaning parents are doing too much for their children rather than helping their children learn independently. Parents so badly want their children to succeed that they often shield them from the inevitable little failures of daily life. For example, parents who are overly involved in their children's homework—organizing, directing, and sometimes even doing it for them—aren't allowing their children to take possession of their own responsibilities. If a child doesn't do well on an assignment or a test, it can be an invaluable learning exercise because we all need experience in how to learn from our mistakes.

We aren't advocating a hands-off approach for all students and parents; indeed, certain children need more supervision and help than others. For example, children who are not self-starters or who have difficulty with organization skills may need their parents to help them get started on homework, persist in the face of frustration, and organize and prioritize. However, children must be the primary agents of their own schoolwork. Children benefit from coping with their feelings of frustration and then working tenaciously toward understanding a difficult question or concept. Also, the child who is not able to understand a concept independently benefits from learning to ask the teacher for an additional explanation. These experiences contribute to the development of frustration tolerance. Failure and disappointment are not merely all right in moderation, they are essential and can actually help build resiliency. There is a body of research that investigates the role of manageable levels of stress on children and finds that low to moderate levels of stress and challenge can serve as stress inoculators, in that they create a template from which children expect to endure and overcome hurdles throughout their lives (Maag & Kotlash, 1994).

A Good Risk-Taker Is Tenacious

Third, a good risk-taker is tenacious. He is able to persist in the face of challenge and hard work because he wants to repeat the feeling he had with a positive outcome. Disappointments and some failures are inevitable in the process of accomplishing a goal. Sometimes the goal is far off, and the child can't readily see the end result in sight; the ability to persist, although the goal is not in one's immediate grasp, is what tenaciousness is about. In the process of being tenacious, good risks are taken. For example, a girl who loves volleyball and finds the sport to be fun and enlivening, sets out to develop her skills. She tells herself that she wants to become a good player, so she joins an after-school club and plays every Friday afternoon. The next year she tries out for the local city team, not knowing whether she's good enough to compete. This is her risk, because she will experience the pain of disappointment if she doesn't make the team. Yet all her work will not be for naught because she can derive satisfaction from playing and improving. And if she makes the team, she has a success in her pocket, which has come from her hard work and persistence.

A Good Risk-Taker Derives Pleasure and Pride in Her Achievements

The final characteristic of a good risk-taker is being able to take realistic pleasure in her achievements. The volleyball player feels good about her achievements, even if she isn't yet on the prestigious city team. She enjoys playing and growing in her skills and competence. She feels more powerful and competent as she achieves higher levels of skill and knowledge about the game. A good risk-taker is realistic about her abilities and knows her strengths and limits. She may dream about one day making the high school team, but knows that presently she is a novice. This takes away neither her enjoyment of the game, nor the pleasure derived from her accomplishments.

INTRODUCTION OF OUR PARENT-CHILD PAIRS

Many of the ideas that we develop and parenting practices that we recommend will be illustrated through vignettes of four parent-child pairs. These pairs represent a collage of the many parents and children whom we've known and worked with over the years. We have chosen four pairs who represent a cross section of the myriad of parent–child pairs that exist. Although these vignettes could not capture the variety of families in our diverse culture, we expect that every parent will find many familiar situations in these prototypical pairings of different temperaments, experiences, parenting styles, and developmental stages.

KATIE AND DYLAN

We intoduced this mother-son pair in the introduction to this book. Katie's parents experienced much loss in their younger years, and as a result discouraged Katie and her siblings from veering from the safe and narrow path. Katie had an artist's sensibility; she was keyed into visual aesthetics and emotionally fine-tuned. She tended to be introspective and shy. She had wanted to pursue a career in the arts, but her parents had discouraged this because of the financial and other instabilities of such a life.

Katie's initial tendency as a young mother was to protect her kids from everything that looked, or felt, risky. She had experienced overprotective parenting and so began to repeat the cycle. Her older son was a resilient and easygoing child who did not challenge or threaten Katie's status quo. Dylan, however, was a more vulnerable child. He was a colicky infant and had difficulty making transitions from early on. His language delays were exacerbated by a mild stammer that

made him more hesitant to join in with his peers in day care and nursery school. Katie and Dylan were in many ways similar. This made
it all the more difficult for Katie to parent Dylan without excessive
worry. Her heart ached for him as he struggled in his verbal expression and social interactions. She knew, though, that he possessed many
strengths: a quiet wit, a creative mind, and a burgeoning talent for
writing. Katie wanted Dylan to be able to go for his dreams in a way
in which she had not been able to do. How was she going to be able
to help Dylan achieve his dreams? How could she separate her own
disappointments and hurdles from the ones he would encounter?

CHARLES AND TIFFANY

We have also already introduced our readers to Charles, an energetic, outgoing, and social man, whose daughter, Tiffany, is by nature
tentative and fearful of new situations. From preschool Tiffany experienced a lot of difficulty establishing friendships. It was clear from
early on that Tiffany's strengths lay in her deep intelligence and keen
mind. Parenting Tiffany was a challenge for Charles because the two of
them were so different. Although Tiffany was emotionally attached to
her parents and enjoyed playing and having fun with them, she shied
away from other children, preferring to be alone rather than socialize. In nursery school she would sit contentedly playing with puzzles,
looking through books, or drawing rather than seeking out social experiences with her peers. In situations with many people, lots of activity, and loud noises, she would become anxious and want to leave. On
the playground, she needed to be coaxed and encouraged to engage
with others. As difficult as it was for Tiffany to make friends, activities
such as reading, drawing, doing puzzles, and looking at maps came
naturally to her.

It was hard enough that Tiffany seemed to be so different from
Charles. To complicate matters, Charles's own childhood was colored
by an overly intrusive mother who pried into every aspect of his life,
from his friends to his schoolwork. If he brought home a bad report
card from school, he was punished severely. Charles learned that failure was humiliating, so he quickly learned to keep his vulnerabilities
and failures to himself. While this emotional stance could at times interfere with his work and interpersonal relationships, Charles often
was able to disguise his insecurities by being the "life of the party."

Charles wondered how, with all of their differences, he could help Tiffany become a good risk-taker in life. He knew how disappointed he felt about his daughter's social difficulties, yet he knew that he didn't want to repeat the same mistakes his mother had made with him. How could he help his daughter go for her dreams?

Louis and Chris

Louis was raised in a family of five children by parents who both worked long hours. Being the oldest child, he was expected to be responsible for the younger children while his parents worked. Louis's parents were loving but strict, and at times punitive if the children didn't behave up to their high expectations. Louis was a serious boy and a good student. He would plan out his homework and study time daily, and finished assignments weeks before they were due. He longed to play on sports teams, but wasn't able to because of his child-care responsibilities. He was angry and resentful about not having the opportunity to do team athletics, but didn't express to his parents how he felt because he was wary of their disappointment. Louis had some difficulties regulating intense feelings, particularly anger, as he grew into adulthood. As a child, he struggled with temper tantrums, and into adolescence he would lose his cool and have verbal tirades when very disappointed. As an adult, he learned how to control these outbursts and rarely behaved inappropriately in work or public settings.

When he became a parent, though, these issues of emotional management came back to haunt him as he tried to give his son, Chris, everything that he hadn't gotten. Chris was, in many ways, different from Louis. Chris was an easygoing, even-tempered, cautious—almost placid—child. An average student and average athlete, he enjoyed sports and school, as he was a naturally social child and enjoyed being with other children.

Louis was often dissatisfied with Chris's easygoing nature, and would become impatient with Chris's "lackadaisical" ways, thinking (and saying) that Chris "would never amount to anything" unless he pushed himself more.

Louis once told a friend, "Man, if I had all the advantages this kid has, I'd be the President of the United States. He doesn't realize how good he has it!"

Louis, too, wanted Chris to be able to go for his dreams. He wondered why his son didn't have the "fire" he had. Did he need to have this fire to be a good risk-taker? Would all of Louis's pushing be helpful or harmful to Chris?

JUDY AND HANNAH

Judy grew up in a suburban town. Her father was a teacher and her mother was a stay-at-home mom. Judy's mother was a devoted and competent woman; however, she was very wary about the physical safety of her only child. She would repeatedly tell her daughter to be careful whenever she played outside, attempted a sport, or even left the house to go to school. As a child, Judy was sensitive, introspective, and bright, and she tended to be anxious in new and uncertain situations. She was also perceptive about people and nurturing to younger children. Temperamentally, Judy was able to calm herself down when upset and entertain herself when she had nothing to do. Throughout her childhood, her mother's worries about her safety exacerbated her own, and she developed a wariness of sports and situations that entailed most physical risk. Judy was a diligent and accomplished student, who derived a great deal of her self-esteem from academic achievements. She spent long hours throughout her childhood and adolescence reading books and escaping into the adventures of literature.

Judy turned her nurturance and love of ideas into becoming a teacher like her father. She had a daughter, Hannah, who was feisty, highly social, and as adventurous as Judy was wary. From the time she could walk, Hannah was running, jumping, and climbing to heights that were not safe, and this frightened her mother. Judy's initial reaction was always to make sure her child was safe. However, this was difficult with a child like Hannah, who craved physical activity.

Hannah was a gifted athlete who began to ice skate at an early age. She loved skating and excelled right away. When Hannah entered school, it was clear that she was more interested in running and jumping than writing her letters and reading. Hannah would become frustrated with activities that involved sitting still, such as practicing writing skills and learning concepts that did not come as easily to her as athletics.

When frustrated by academics or any impasse to her immediate needs, such as not being given cookies before dinner, she would protest intensely and have a tantrum. Sometimes she would throw things, scream, and slam her door hard. It was difficult for her to rebound from her frustration, and although she needed structure and limits, she also needed patience and soothing from her mother. Judy also wanted to help Hannah follow her dreams. How was Judy going to manage to navigate the narrow line between nurturance and setting firm limits for Hannah? How was she going to manage to raise this daring girl who was so different from herself?

LEARNING THE POWER OF RISK: BEGINNING A RISK JOURNAL

We know that it is important for us, as parents, to take an active role in guiding our children toward taking good risks. One way to do this is to begin a "risk journal." A risk journal is an ongoing compilation of your experiences, thoughts, feelings, and reactions about your child's risk-taking style and development. Writing in a journal reserved solely for understanding your child's risk-taking development can solidify the insights and behavioral changes that can take place. Noting, for example, how difficult it is for you to enforce a time-out when your 3-year-old repeatedly throws a toy at a friend may be an important facet of understanding yourself, your child, and her risk-taking style. If you felt sorry for your 3-year-old, who was sobbing in the corner, and also embarrassed that she had struck your best friend's son, you are beginning to do the work that leads to understanding and change. Writing in a journal can help you become more aware of your long-standing attitudes and parenting philosophies and, concurrently, can help you identify the ways in which, for example, you cope with strong feelings. It can also help you see your child's behavior and the interactions between your child and you more clearly.

Throughout the book we insert brief quotes from parent journals so our readers understand the process of self-reflection, self-doubt, insight, and sometimes humor that are part of a risk journal. For example, here is a brief excerpt from the first pages of Charles's journal. In this entry he was referring to the experience in which he was patiently attempting to help Tiffany take more risks on the playground:

That whole experience in the playground this morning was a bust. Tif was finally getting it, and then this overconfident kid comes by and scares her all over again. . . and that Mom, she only made the whole thing worse. Thinking about it, I guess I did all right by Tif by not lashing out at that Mom, but I wanted to. . . . And she did go down the slide—that was a step forward for her.

PRAGMATIC STEPS TOWARD THOUGHTFUL RISK-TAKING

There are four concrete and pragmatic steps that lead to good risk-taking:

1. Identifying a risk, which can be physical, emotional, social or intellectual, or a combination of factors
2. Staying aware of both the potential dangers and benefits of moving forward or staying still
3. Thinking through one's actions
4. Evaluating one's actions afterward.

Risk, like all skills, also entails repetition and practice. Another vignette about Charles and Tiffany illustrates these steps and demonstrates how Charles helps his daughter, now a third grader, learn to speak up in class through practicing these steps.

CHARLES AND TIFFANY'S STORY

Tiffany was reluctant to take the risk to speak up in a classroom setting. She had trouble understanding the intricacies of social relationships and this exacerbated her difficulty in speaking up, even though she often had many thoughts and ideas.

Tiffany's teachers had been encouraging her to speak up in class and join in class discussions. During parent-teacher conferences they told her parents that she was shy and reticent in class and that she needed more confidence in her ability to contribute to the class learning process. Tiffany wanted to feel more a part of things, but was fearful of the risks involved. She worried that she would "sound stupid," or would be ridiculed by her peers or teacher.

When she was in third grade, her Dad started conversations with her to see if he could help her speak up in class. Sometimes their talks were productive; at other times, Tiffany would retreat in tears, and Charles in frustration and anger. They managed, though, to talk about what held her back from raising her hand. Together, they imagined the worst-case scenario; what would that be like for her?

"Awful," Tiffany said.
"But you would survive, right?" Charles asked.
"Barely," answered Tiffany.
With this they both laughed.

Conversations like these went a long way for Tiffany. Even though she still couldn't actually get up the courage to speak in class, she came to realize that the risk wasn't as devastating as she had imagined.

At other times, Charles and Tiffany imagined how she would feel if she raised her hand to contribute an idea to a class discussion. What if another student made fun of her? They talked about why some kids need to make fun of others, and how this was a sign that the person felt insecure and perhaps bad about himself. Once, Charles told Tiffany that when he was in third grade, he would sometimes be the one who made fun of other kids. Tiffany listened to his stories, enraptured. He told Tiffany that he now understands that he did this to make himself feel better—to try to prove, to himself and to others, that he was really stronger than he felt.

As the months went on, Tiffany became ready to try out speaking— just a little—in class. Charles recruited her teacher, and they developed a plan that would make this easier for her. They decided together that Tiffany would answer a specific question that the two of them had prearranged the day before. This went exceedingly well, and Tiffany felt very successful. Several days later, though, when Tiffany gathered the courage to raise her hand and speak up without a specific plan— and no words came out. She was mortified and left the classroom in tears. Luckily, with an understanding teacher and father, Tiffany was able to recover from this embarrassment. In fact, several days later she and Charles even joked—a bit—about the worst-case scenario having actually happened.

Over time, there were steps forward and backward. There were more tears and triumphs along the way. Supported by her parents and teachers, Tiffany was able to slowly make strides toward being a more active participant in class and learn that she could also survive failure and humiliation.

On Charles's side, he realized, initially, that he was irritated, impatient, and embarrassed by Tiffany's passivity. He and his wife decided to consult with the school social worker to help them help Tiffany. Charles noticed his desire to push Tiffany into being someone that she wasn't and was encouraged by his wife and the professionals around him to be aware of his own needs and feelings and not act on them. This wasn't easy for Charles, but he, like his daughter, kept persevering. In a journal entry an irritated Charles wrote, "I am not cut out for this kind of stuff. But when Tif and I could actually laugh about her worst fear happening . . . it just took the sting out for both of us."

How did Charles practice each pragmatic step in this illustration? First, he helped Tiffany identify the particular risk being approached: raising her hand and speaking up in class. This risk is comprised of a combination of social, emotional, and intellectual factors for Tiffany. Since she has difficulty reading social cues, she was afraid that she would misunderstand what was expected of her and thus would be chastised (by the teacher) or ridiculed (by the children). Tiffany also had to tolerate the strong feelings of uncertainty and anxiety as she prepared to participate in class. Learning to speak up in class is also an intellectual risk for her because she feared that she couldn't articulate her thoughts clearly.

The second step was that Charles and Tiffany's ongoing discussions kept her aware of the dangers and benefits of raising her hand and speaking versus staying quiet. Considering the alternatives in any given situation is an essential part of learning how to size up risks and make decisions on how to proceed as you confront them. The danger to Tiffany was putting herself in the spotlight, something that is uncomfortable for her.

Talking about these topics with her father and others, and playacting or role playing, helped Tiffany to think through her actions, the third step toward good risk-taking. (In Chapter 7 we discuss in detail the rudiments of role playing and other activities that are useful for thinking through risk-taking actions.)

Finally, Charles and Tiffany evaluated their actions. This can sometimes be accomplished in a lighthearted way. For example, after Tiffany recovered from the embarrassment of "not even getting a word out," they were able to joke about it. Tiffany could laugh when her father said, "Well, at least the sky didn't come tumbling down on you. I guess it could have been worse!" This vignette illustrates that learning good risk-taking requires time and practice. Over time, Tiffany, like other children, continued to have both successful and unsuccessful experiences in the classroom.

SUMMING UP

In this chapter we have introduced our readers to our concept of risk. We have defined it from a perspective that is rooted in child development, placed it within a historical context, and delineated the major components and pragmatic steps involved. We have also introduced our four parent-child pairs who will appear throughout the book. We hope that the parents and teachers who are reading this book will use our words and suggested activities to guide themselves and their children toward practicing good risk-taking so that, in Eleanor Roosevelt's words, they can "taste [life's] experience to the utmost, [and] reach out eagerly . . . for newer and richer experiences."

Chapter 2

CHILD DEVELOPMENT AND RISK-TAKING

The dangers of life are infinite and among them is safety.

—*Goethe*

To become good risk-takers children need to become more adept at leaving their equilibrium—their places of comfort—to go toward something that may be scary or daunting, in an attempt to try something new. As our children practice risk-taking skills, they are also becoming more resilient (tolerating failure and bouncing back from difficult times), more internally motivated (thriving on the feeling of accomplishment), and more confident (Coleman & Hagell, 2006). In other words, children who are good risk-takers tend to soar because they believe, "I can do it!"

Sociologists and social workers who are interested in understanding the interplay between development and culture have studied the relationship between risk and resilience. Mark Fraser (2004) and his colleagues examine the effects of negative risks, such as poverty, harsh parenting, and parental conflict, on the child's resilience—in Fraser's words, her ability to "overcome the odds." More specifically, he defines *resilience* as "the attainment of positive outcomes despite high-risk status" (p. 23). Fraser has found that some children have the ability to remain strong despite adverse or difficult situations. Some researchers have found—unexpectedly—that exposure to risk actually can increase a child's resilience (Werner & Smith, 1992). Fraser asserts, though, that while children have a wide variety of responses to stressors, it is now known that children who are exposed to highly negative stress factors are not necessarily more adaptive or resilient than other children. In fact, recent studies have shown that it is a complex combination of temperamental, environmental, and family variables that contribute to a child's ability to maintain tenacity—to remain resilient—in a difficult situation (Fraser, Kirby & Smokowski, 2004). So, the belief that the school of hard knocks is good for children is not true. But, while exposure to negative risk is harmful, practicing good risk-taking does build resilience. The development of resilience—landing on one's feet in the face of adversity—is definitely a good thing, and some children are naturally more resilient than others. Children respond differently in the face of stress. We have found that most children become more resilient as they practice taking good risks.

In this chapter we discuss six fundamental risks that span development. We also describe the risks that are specific to each developmental stage. First, though, it will be helpful to present a brief overview of child development.

OVERVIEW OF CHILD DEVELOPMENT

Since the early twentieth century, clinicians and academicians have sought to better understand the social, emotional, and intellectual growth process of the child from infancy to adulthood. As Sigmund Freud (1915–1917/1963) created a model that explained the workings of the human mind, he also developed a model of psychosexual development of the child, which included the oral, anal, genital, and oedipal stages (Freud, 1915–1917/1963). Later generations of psychoanalysts, including Anna Freud (1965, 1968), Melanie Klein (1923), Erik Erikson (1950), and Margaret Mahler (1968, 1975) continued to expand upon the ways in which children psychologically develop. Jean Piaget (1998) spent his professional life observing and writing about the child's stages of intellectual growth. He provided a new paradigm to the field of psychology in terms of understanding the stages of children's cognitive growth. Another key theoretician who categorized intellectual thought in children was Gesell (1946, 1955, 1956). Psychologists today continue to work toward understanding better the ins and outs of how a child grows. It is key that parents understand the rudiments of child development so they have a better understanding of—and perhaps more tolerance for—behaviors that can be associated with each stage of development. For example, in our clinical practices parents often ask us questions such as "My 2-year-old has developed sleep difficulties for the first time. Why, and is this normal?" Or "My 3-year-old is hitting and biting other children. Is this normal?" Being educated in the knowledge of our children's development gives us the perspective, as parents, to respond to our children with greater patience, objectivity, understanding, and empathy.

Development Varies with the Individual

Parents also need to understand that the stages of child development are fluid and vary with the individual. It is usual, for example, for a typical 11-year-old to show some behaviors typical of a "tween" (ages 10 to 12), such as having an interest in popular music and teenage clothing, but this same child will likely not yet be ready or interested in exploring romantic interests in the opposite sex. One 11- or 12-year-old may not at all be interested in popular culture, fashion, or romance, while another may in fact be quite interested. This is completely normal. We share this knowledge with the hope that it will help parents to feel more relaxed—not more anxious—about their child's development. We suggest that parents use the information we impart with the intent to increase the understanding of your child and your relationship with him. It is helpful to keep in mind the following guidelines while thinking about child development:

- Carefully observe your child's behaviors and actions over the period of a week. What do you notice about her central interests, behaviors, and actions? How are these typical of her age group?
- Do you observe consistent strengths or consistent problem areas? For example, does your 5- or 6-year-old still have difficulty separating from mom or dad when he enters the classroom? While this is a typical behavior of a 3-year-old, it is important for the parent of a 6-year-old who continues to have separation difficulties to understand why this behavior remains.
- What can you learn (from your parents/relatives) about your own development as a child? Were you obstinate or easygoing? Did you throw temper tantrums? How was your development similar to or different from your child's? As we will show in subsequent chapters, gaining knowledge about yourself is an important part of the process of understanding your current perspective on your child's behavior.

Seven Stages of Development

Based on years of experience and the observation of many children and their families, as well as studying the work of clinicians and theorists before us, we divide child development into seven stages. Unlike some earlier theoreticians, though, we propose that these stages are neither absolute nor unchangeable. Our seven stages of childhood are as follows:

Birth to 3s: From Us to Me. A child is born with the ability to perceive (see, hear, feel, touch, smell) and to connect emotionally with another human being. Furthermore, while the infant's brain and nervous system is rudimentary at birth, it grows more during these years than at any other time in life. It is during the first three years that the foundations for learning about relationships, learning how to move about in this world and learning language develop. The child is, at first, completely dependent on the parent, and as she develops the ability to crawl, toddle, and understand and express language, she develops a sense of autonomy. During this time the infant moves from thinking that she and her caregiver are one (see Mahler, 1968; Mahler, Pine, & Bergman, 1975; Stern, 1985), to emerging as a separate entity from the caregiver. In this process, the child becomes aware that she is separate from her parent, yet she doesn't understand that parents go away— for a short time—and then come back. This causes normal anxiety for the child. When, for example, the 9- to 12-month-old is afraid to let a stranger hold him, he is expressing this normal developmental unease.

3 to 5 (Preschool): Entering the World Beyond Mommy and Daddy. The preschooler has mastered (or is in the process of mastering) the developmental tasks of infancy: walking, talking, grasping objects, communicating basic needs, and developing a trusting relationship with a caregiver (and possibly siblings and other family members). The brain and nervous system continue to develop, and the preschooler becomes interested in the world around her. Intellectual curiosity grows. The child wants to hear stories read aloud; she shows increased interest in numbers, shapes, and colors. The preschooler is also continuing to regulate her body and is mastering toilet training. She is especially curious about her own body and may be curious about her friend's bodies, especially the difference between boys and girls. It is at this time that children begin to learn right from wrong and begin to feel empathy toward another person. Most important, though, this stage is characterized by the importance of learning to negotiate and interact with one's peers. Children are often in day care or in preschool settings for at least a part of the day and thus are together with other children. In these settings outside the home, young children are learning to share, become members of groups, follow directions, and play interactively.

5 to 10 (Primary School): The Age of Mastery. The early primary-school-age child is becoming a complex and competent being. He continues to form deeper and more involved relationships with peers (more often but not always with the same sex), and is also immersed in family relationships. Often (but not always) children in this age group develop a best friend or group of best friends. Physically, the 5- to 9-year-old child is becoming stronger and more physically coordinated. During this stage children may become interested in trying out for individual or team sports, playing a musical instrument, drawing, or acting. By the end of this stage, children have acquired the basic academic skills of reading, math, and writing, and they take pleasure in mastering these concepts, skills, and facts, as well as pleasing their teachers and parents.

Although the focus of this book is on children ages 3 through 10, the preschooler through the primary-school-age child, we believe it is helpful for parents to understand the developmental steps of the entire scope of childhood in order to have a working knowledge of what's ahead. Therefore, we will describe the basic needs and tasks of the preteen and adolescent stages.

10 to 13 (Late Primary School/Middle School): Tweens—The Age of Curiosity. "What's happening to my child?" the parent of a tween or preteen often wonders. One's largely predictable, eager to please 9-year-old has turned into an unpredictable and thorny 10-year-old. The physical development of puberty, which takes place over several years and in several stages (Madaras, 2007) brings on rapid physical, psychological, and social changes (Levy-Warren, 1996). Hormonal changes affect daily behavior, and tweens' interests shift rapidly. Tweens become interested in popular culture and feel the need to conform to their peers' standards of dress and behavior. Many tweens begin to explore their sexual identity.

Two central thrusts are prominent in this stage. First, there is a shift away from family toward the peer group. Second, there is significant intellectual growth: At about 12 years of age, the tween is able to think and reason abstractly. This has important implications for his growth as an independent human being. The tween has less interest in mastering facts and figures than his younger counterparts. He begins to become more interested in debating larger world issues. The tween, who seems often to care more about what his friends think than what his parents and teachers think, tends to worry less about pleasing his parents and teachers. Much like the toddler, the tween is beginning a new separation—from his family and from his childhood (Blos, 1967). In years past, children on the younger end of this stage (age 9 to 11) were still considered to be rooted in latency and the emergence of interest in sexuality and popular culture occurred in the teenage years. This change is most likely due to a combination of factors including the increasingly powerful effect of the media and Internet in exposing younger children to more information, and a trend for girls to reach menses at an earlier age than in past generations. (The average age of first menstruation is now 12 years old instead of 13.) Earlier physical development brings with it earlier hormonal shifts, along with the resulting behavioral and emotional behaviors of adolescence.

13 to 15 (Early Adolescence): I am My Peer Group. The early adolescent continues the tasks of the tween. As the adolescent's body matures, she continues to explore her sexual identity. For some children, romantic relationships begin to burgeon; for others, romantic interests are felt and thought about, but not acted on. During this stage, the peer group remains central. The adolescent is in a quest for developing his identity in all sorts of ways—who he is as a student and as a member of the peer group, the community, and the family. In this process the young adolescent often questions his parents' values and rules and society's norms. This process of questioning is promoted by the increased ability to think abstractly. The young adolescent often develops a particular skill, talent, or passion. For instance, this is the time when a young adolescent might sit for hours in his room playing his guitar, listening to indie music, or skateboarding with friends.

15 to 17 (Middle Adolescence): The Age of Passions. The 15- to 17-year-old is typically a passionate being. Her ability to think and reason abstractly and to feel deeply sets the stage for the middle adolescent to develop strong passions of all kinds, from academics to politics, from sports to the arts, from romantic relationships to religion. Commonly, and importantly, these interests and passions are distinct from her parents'. With increased sophistication, the adolescent is continuing to define herself as a separate being from her family. Often, the 15- to 17-year-old becomes increasingly independent and begins to explore and sometimes establish intimate and sexual relationships.

18+ (Late Adolescence): The Reemergence of Me. Late adolescence (which can extend through the twenties) is characterized by the consolidation of many of the developmental themes of earlier adolescence. As the adolescent leaves his parent's home and enters either a work environment or university, he begins to establish a sense of himself as an adult—hopefully, someone who is capable of having meaningful (and lasting) long-term intimate relationships, is productive and creative in the workplace (or university), and is empathic and connected to family, community, and the greater world. This process, of course, is never complete. These thrusts become lifelong challenges for all of us. Erik Erikson (1950) was very much aware of this challenge, as well as the risks involved in moving to the next stage of development. He wrote, "The strength acquired at any stage is tested by the necessity to transcend it in such a way that the individual can take chances in the next stage with what was most vulnerably precious in the previous one" (p. 263).

THE IMPORTANCE OF UNDERSTANDING DEVELOPMENT

With a greater understanding and appreciation of the process of development, a parent is better equipped to accept and tolerate the vicissitudes of a child's development. If, for example, you are shopping with your 9-year-old, and she asks to buy a distinctive (but, in your opinion, unattractive) hat and then decides to wear it every day, you can understand that this is a natural part of her growth. She is beginning to (both literally and metaphorically) try on new looks and identities. This behavior, while seemingly odd to you, is completely appropriate. If you are driving your 10-year-old son to soccer practice and he asks you to change the radio dial to the hip-hop station, you shouldn't be surprised. This is an indication that your preadolescent wants to be in with the latest in popular culture.

Furthermore, a parent who understands the rudiments of development is better able to understand the typical risks—both good and bad—that emerge from each stage. For example, the preschooler mostly deals with risks about separating from a primary caregiver for the first time. If your 3- or 4-year-old cries when you leave him at nursery school, this is a typical emotional reaction. A central risk at this stage is to tolerate the strong feelings conjured up by being apart from one's parent. In contrast, the 6- or 7-year-old's risks are often associated with mastering expectations in the classroom. Your second-grader who feels some anxiety when he reads aloud in class, but forges ahead anyway, is taking a typical and smart risk for a child of that age.

Erikson noted the risks involved in moving from one stage to the next; moving from safe and comfortable ground to the unfamiliar accentuates our human vulnerabilities. But without this movement, there is stagnation. Regardless of age or stage, there are universal emotional risks that most children tackle in order to progress developmentally. Emotional risks can be subtle and easy to miss. Yet, they underlie many important steps we take in life.

WHAT ARE UNIVERSAL EMOTIONAL RISKS?

While specific risks vary from individual to individual and from age to age, there are fundamental psychological and emotional risks that span development. These risks, unlike the challenging physical risks that Lyng (2005) discusses, place the individual on a subjective precipice between emotional danger and safety. Someone else may not know that you are taking an emotional risk, but you can feel it intensely. Furthermore, while we can sometimes get an adrenaline rush from experiencing our accomplishment, this is not the central impetus of taking an emotional risk. We attempt them to move closer to our goals, to move ahead in life. Although some children are born with a tendency toward taking risks, everyone can practice and master good emotional risk-taking. In fact, the child who is wired from birth to take risks, or who tends to be impulsive, may or may not become a thoughtful risk-taker. Conversely, the child who is naturally cautious or risk-avoidant may learn to develop a good risk-taking style. In subsequent chapters, we discuss the factors of temperamental endowment, learning style, and parent-child relationship, all of which impact on risk-taking style.

The following list outlines universal emotional risks and common feelings associated with taking these risks. Throughout our lives we are taking these risks knowingly and unknowingly. While most people regard these as simply goals to reach during development, they are also, in our view, universal risks. Mastering them propels us forward, but not without grappling with sometimes extremely uncomfortable feelings of our human vulnerability and possible failure. These are risks because there is a struggle, which can be frightening and painful. Withdrawal from this struggle may seem to be the safer way to go, yet risk avoidance usually leads to stagnation

Finally, while each of these risks is significant in and of itself, in our daily life one risk can be hard to distinguish from another. For example, the risk of mastery may require simultaneously risking delayed gratification.

Six Risks and Associated Feelings

1. The risk of achievement and mastery
   A. Positive feeling: self-esteem
   B. Negative feeling: incompetence
2. The risk of separation from the primary caregiver
   A. Positive feelings: independence, autonomy
   B. Negative feelings: loneliness, aloneness
3. The risk of enduring delayed gratification
   A. Positive feelings: self-control, frustration tolerance, personal power
   B. Negative feelings: deprivation, frustration, powerlessness
4. The risk of social and emotional connection with others
   A. Positive feelings: closeness, intimacy, social confidence, being known by others
   B. Negative feelings: rejection, isolation, criticism
5. The risk of expressing one's beliefs, convictions, knowledge, and ideas
   A. Positive feelings: self-expression, self-assertion, self-confidence
   B. Negative feelings: disapproval, denigration, and humiliation
6. The risk of struggling with uncertainty
   A. Positive feelings: ability to self-soothe (calm oneself), freedom and confidence to take on new challenges
   B. Negative feelings: unease, anxiety

Taking the Risk to Achieve and to Master

Achievement, whether in the form of mastery or accomplishment, can be a potent medicine. Success in accomplishing a goal results in feelings of increased competence and self-esteem. One success builds upon another, and over time this process strengthens our child's sense of confidence in his abilities. The child who feels successful enjoys this feeling and repeats it. So he tends to persevere through challenges.

What, then, is risky about achievement? Every time a child takes a risk to achieve, he also takes a chance of failing. While we know that failure is an inevitable part of taking any risk, failing at something can result in feeling incompetent, frustrated, unworthy, and self-deprecated. For example, when a 7-year-old boy attempts to work on his math homework (let's suppose that math doesn't come easily to this child) and can't figure out the placement of the tens, hundreds, and thousands columns, he can feel pretty frustrated. If he has encountered other difficulties in his academics, and if his older sister gets straight As in math and has received praise from his parents, he may feel especially incompetent and anxious. To persist with his homework or to ask someone to help explain it to him is to risk experiencing uncomfortable feelings of uncertainty; and he still risks the possibility of failure despite these efforts. If this child fails after trying his best, this still constitutes a good risk—a move toward growth.

Taking the Risk to Separate

Children often face—and struggle through—their strongest feelings and thoughts when they are apart from their parents. This can be hard to tolerate. If being alone is an uncomfortable risk, then why bother taking it at all? The flip side is that being able to function—to learn and have fun—without mommy or daddy present, results in increased independence and the appreciation for the relationships we have, as well as increased confidence. Furthermore, research and practice has shown that the ability to be alone fosters an increased capacity for creativity (Winnicott, 1958). It is during these alone times that the child has the freedom to think and create in a fully uninhibited way. Children who always need to be with others and be entertained by parents, peers, television, or computer lose out on the experience of spending time by themselves. When your child reads a book, thinks, daydreams, draws, or pursues other independent interests, she is developing important internal capacities for independence, creativity, and comfort. This is an important capacity for children to develop in the pursuit of healthy psychological separation from their parents.

Taking the Risk to Wait

Like the other goals we discuss, being able to delay gratification can feel frustrating and uncomfortable. The 3-year-old who does not get the candy she wants—"now!"—may be so upset and frustrated that she melts down into a temper tantrum. If she doesn't get the sweet, she risks losing the real and anticipated pleasure of eating the candy. Perhaps more important, she risks feeling powerless and small, since her parent is in control of the outcome and is preventing her from having what she wants. The delay of gratification can also be seen in the case of the second grader who can't control her impulses to shout out the answer in class. Struggling with impulse control is not only the work of young children. It is a lifelong process that is a part of learning to delay gratification, and is part of a healthy risk-taking style. By delaying gratification, we can think through our desires, needs, and impulses, and weigh out the costs and benefits of an action. This gives us an increased sense of mastery and personal power (power that is used productively and positively) and increases the potential of feeling competent, socially skilled, successful, and happy. The second grader who can hold on to her thoughts and raise her hand in class may or may not get called on by the teacher. She will feel frustration if not recognized by the teacher, but she also will not be chastised for her impulsivity, and this will lead to benefits of all kinds, including self-respect, better social standing, and positive regard from the teacher. Such rewards, when felt by the child, lead to more and more desire to control immediate impulses and are the seeds of a larger sense of personal control.

JUDY AND HANNAH'S STORY

When Hannah was very young she had great difficulty waiting to have something that she badly wanted. If Judy and Hannah would pass an ice-cream store or a bakery while walking around town, Hannah would inevitably want her mother to take her into the store and buy her a dessert. Of course, this wasn't always possible because sometimes they were in a hurry to get somewhere, or it was an inappropriate time of day to have dessert. Hannah would persist when Judy would say no: "I want a chocolate chip cookie! Now!" the 3-year-old Hannah would shout loudly.

When Judy tried to hold her ground, Hannah would often continue to escalate in her request for the cookie, getting louder and throwing a tantrum. Sometimes it was just easier for Judy to negotiate with Hannah, for example, by buying the cookie with the proviso that Hannah could eat it later. This would sometimes work in avoiding a full-blown tantrum, and sometimes it wouldn't. Judy was disturbed by this pattern and decided that Hannah needed to learn to accept the word *no* and learn that her desires and impulses could not always be met exactly when she wanted.

Judy began to stick more firmly to her decisions with Hannah even when she knew Hannah would be displeased and frustrated. The next time that Hannah asked to turn on the television to watch a cartoon during dinner, Judy told her that she could watch TV after dinner, but not during.

"I want to watch SpongeBob SquarePants," Hannah wailed.
"There's no TV during dinner, Hannah. You know that. You'll have to wait until we're finished," Judy replied calmly but firmly.
Hannah escalated into a full-blown tantrum, to which Judy responded as calmly as she could, repeating that she knew that this upset Hannah, but that she would have to wait until after dinner.
The first few times Judy stayed firm, she was met with loud protests. When Hannah finally calmed down, Judy hugged her, and initiated a conversation with her about waiting for things.
"I know it's *so* hard to wait for something or not get something that you want so badly," Judy began.
"I think you're being mean, mean, mean!" Hannah responded.
"You may think this, Hannah, but I carefully think about these decisions, and I decide what's best for you because you're still a little girl. Sometimes you get to choose things, but sometimes you have to listen to me or other grown-ups and not get what you want, at the exact moment you want it. This makes you angry, I know. You're allowed to feel whatever feeling you have, but you need to learn how to wait and how to control your outbursts."
"How?" Hannah asked in a surprisingly quiet voice.
"I will help you with this," Judy replied.

Hannah continued to have difficulty with her frustration tolerance. However, it improved over time as she learned that her insistence was not rewarded. She also wanted her mother's approval and wanted to feel successful, so she worked very hard to talk herself down when she was frustrated or angry, just as her mother talked to her. Hannah learned to delay her gratification better and better as she developed greater emotional and cognitive maturity.

Taking the Risk to Connect

While most children first learn about forming close relationships through their earliest connections with their parents and siblings, it can be a risky endeavor for children to put themselves out there to form close relationships with their peers. If they are ignored or rejected by a peer, they can feel isolated, lonely, and even humiliated.

In contrast, if the risk leads to success—to a connection with a friend—the child experiences new social confidence, and the pleasure of knowing and being known by others. When a 5-year-old kindergartner ventures over to the group of boys and girls who are engaged in building with blocks and says, "Can I play too?" he is taking a risk with his self-esteem. A naturally outgoing child might not be fazed by a negative answer from one or more of the children. He might say to himself, "Oh well, I'll go over to the drawing table." However, for many children this is not an easy thing to say, and a rejection can hurt. The child may be coping with feelings of embarrassment or isolation. If the child takes the risk, he is either included in the play or is told no. Either way he benefits in that he has learned an important lesson about perseverance.

Likewise, when a 10-year-old girl extends herself in friendship to the new girl in her class and asks her if she wants to get together over the weekend, she is taking a risk. The potential cost is rejection, including the sad or angry feelings that go with it. On the other hand, the potential benefit is learning the pleasure of generosity toward others. She is not only making a new friend, but she also learns that she has the capabilities and skills to help another person feel at ease and to create positive, fun experiences for both of them.

Taking the Risk of Self-Expression

The expression of one's beliefs, convictions, and ideas, can be very risky. It can feel dangerous to put one's ideas out publicly, and risk disapproval, denigration, or humiliation. In school with peers or a group of peers or even in the home, a child can receive insensitive criticism. Expressing ideas that are unpopular, or even controversial, can potentially lead to ostracism from the group. Yet personal expression is a risk of cost-benefit. A 9-year-old child at a group playdate in which the girls are discussing favorite new pop singers may ask herself, "How will my ideas be received by others? Is it worth it to express my own opinion, my own musical taste, even though it's different from the others?" For the most part, children who have a basic sense of trust in other people (Erikson, 1950) will find a way to say what they mean when it is important to them, and this is a vital learning experience for all children as well.

In certain situations our beliefs won't be met with support or approval; however, we all need to ferret out the importance of our self-expression in each particular situation. Sometimes keeping one's thoughts to oneself is the smart thing to do. At other times we need to speak up despite other's disapproval. A 10-year-old boy, having watched the televised presidential debates at home with his parents, listened to his friend's family talk about their perspective on the candidates. The boy offered his opinions, which were very different, and went on to criticize the candidate whom this family supported. He was met with an icy silence, which made him feel very uncomfortable. He wondered if he should have just kept his own thoughts to himself.

Developing the ability to size up a situation and ascertain how important it is—that's the difficult task. Children who can develop this skill and use it intelligently develop an increased sense of inner strength and confidence.

Taking the Risk to Struggle with Uncertainty

Most people, children included, feel most comfortable when they are certain of their views and feelings. We have discussed how the expression of controversial beliefs is in itself risky. Struggling with uncertainty, though, goes beyond the risk of self-expression. For example, the child who easily answers a question in class when she is certain of the answer is actively participating and thus growing and learning, but is not necessarily taking a risk. The child who is *not* sure that he has the right answer, yet still expresses his views is taking an important intellectual and emotional risk that can lead to greater achievement, confidence, and the ability to persevere. Why? This is because as the child ventures into uncertain terrain he will stretch his knowledge and emotional capacities. This may mean that his answer is correct, incorrect, or is potentially another angle on the concept. The unexpected answer can generate interesting debate and discussion. Even with an incorrect answer, the child opens an opportunity to better understand his misconception and can learn the concept anew. Children need to learn how to make mistakes and feel okay doing it. It is very important to allow yourself to make a mistake, and to realize that it's not so terrible to be wrong.

From our clinical practices we have observed that it is not only children who have difficulty weathering the feelings associated with being wrong. As one parent said recently, "Neither my husband nor I ever want to be wrong, so how can we expect our children to tolerate their failures, large and small?"

There are many different ways that children struggle with uncertainty. In general, though, the ability to grapple with uncertain feelings or intellectual concepts despite emotional discomfort leads to resiliency of character. This is because the child learns to calm himself, or self-soothe, thereby tolerating temporary discomfort. A 3-year-old entering preschool may self-soothe by bringing her favorite stuffed animal along with her to class in the first few weeks. A shy 6-year-old who raises his hand to answer a question in class self-soothes by thinking about the words his mother said to him the night before: "Just go for it, take a leap!" These different strategies help children think clearly and better manage or regulate their emotions.

Children use the emotional skills they've learned from their parents. If your child has experienced security, consistency, and nurturance at home and if he has learned that he can trust his parents to protect him, he will tend to be able to rely on his teachers and eventually on himself. In adjusting to school the child learns important lessons about coping with uncertainty and how to accept soothing and reassurance from his teacher.

As children get older, the positive risks they take often involve "staying the course" in new or challenging environments and situations. Through taking these risks they learn that struggling with uncertainty usually pays off in growth and learning.

HOW RISK-TAKING UNFOLDS WITH DEVELOPMENT

The seven stages of child development, which we discussed earlier in this chapter, require different goals, or developmental tasks (Anna Freud, 1962; 1988). In addition, certain risks emerge according to a child's developmental stage. In this book we focus on the second and third stages of development—children from preschool through primary school (ages 3 through 10). We focus on these stages because this is when children are ready to begin learning and interacting with the world beyond home. They are still quite young and are at a particularly formative stage of their life. In these years parents, teachers, and others can have an especially significant impact on how children approach security and risk.

In the second stage of development, "Entering the world beyond mommy and daddy (3 to 5)," children's development of language, thought, fine and gross motor control, and social and emotional skills flourish. They learn from living with parents and family, from modeling others' behavior, playing with toys, pretending, and being with other children. They also venture out of the home and into day care and preschool, thus learning to separate from parent and home. These developmental tasks allow them to become more independent, as well as to learn and to have fun inside and outside the home—even when mommy or daddy is away. Activities such as drawing, solving puzzles, games of hide-and-seek, fantasy play with dolls and dress-up clothes help boys and girls learn about themselves and the world around them, and are vehicles for self-expression.

Therefore, the key risks that arise for children during this stage of development involve leaving mommy and daddy and entering the outside world and trying out one's hand at new skills. It can be scary to separate from those you've depended on. Children don't yet know they can survive without their parents. There is risk to standing on one's own two feet outside the home—at day care or at nursery school.

Concurrently, the 3- to 5-year-old child has the increased brain power to struggle with mastery and to experience the frustration, anger, and other feelings that come with being unable to solve a puzzle or draw a person. He learns the pride of physical self-control through activities such as toilet training, but experiences frustration as he learns that he cannot always get what he wants "now."

Social interactions also become increasingly important as the preschooler begins to reap the satisfaction of interacting with peers. Yet for some, if not all, children the risk of social rejection also looms. Children of this age also struggle with uncertainty—the uncertainty of whether mommy will be on time at pickup or whether he can climb to the top of the slide without falling. The 3- to 5-year-old also experiences humiliation and disapproval when he disappoints a parent or other loving adult.

TABLE 2.1. Common Risks for 3- to 5-year-olds

Types of Risk	Good Risks	Poor Risks
Mastery	Drawing a person Learning the ABC song Riding a tricycle	Scribbling on the wall Not participating during music time Running across the street alone
Separation	Attending day care Going to grandma's overnight	Not engaging in school Refusing to leave mommy's side
Delayed gratification	Not getting it "now"	Tantruming until getting it
Social connection	Playing with a new friend	Hitting another child
Expression	Making up silly words to a song	Not singing
Struggling with uncertainty	Trying a new food	Refusing to try new foods; being a picky eater

Table 2.1 illustrates common risks for 3- to 5-year-olds. For each type of risk we list examples of good and poor risk-taking. Note that there could be some overlap among these categories. For example, waiting for mom at pickup time at nursery school entails tolerating delayed gratification as well as learning to cope with the uncertainty of life. At times, what looks like a good risk may actually be a bad risk and vice versa. For example, if parents allowed a child to scribble on the living room walls prior to a paint job, this could become a good risk, helping an anxious, highly controlled, compliant child deal with a stressful change to his environment.

In the third stage, "The age of mastery" (6 to 10), children are focused on developing academic and social skills in the classroom and on the schoolyard, so central risks take place on these two fronts. Table

TABLE 2.2. Common Risks for 5-to 10-year-olds

Types of Risk	Good Risks	Poor Risks
Mastery	Learning the names of the U.S. presidents Joining a community soccer league	Not studying for the history test Not going out for a desired sport
Separation	Going to sleep-away camp	Refusing to go on a school trip
Delayed gratification	Waiting one's turn in line Waiting to be called on in class	Pushing ahead in line Calling out the answer in class
Social connection	Asking a new friend over	Gossiping about the new kid
Expression	Writing a story on a creative theme Expressing fears about reading aloud in a group	Copying another's idea for a story Telling another child her idea is stupid
Struggling with uncertainty	Auditioning for the travel soccer team	Not even trying, even though it is something the child wants

2.2 shows risks for 6- to 10-year-olds. Learning to read, write, do math, and build a reserve of information about the world requires openness to learning and a desire to become competent and proficient. Children need to pay attention in class and learn to discipline their work habits. They struggle with organizing backpacks, books, and papers, and they learn how to settle down to do homework in the evening.

Children of this age also like nothing more than to please their parents and teachers, and to show off their new skills, talents, and abilities to them. Key risks of this age revolve around these tasks. Central for the 6- to 10-year-old child is the risk to master and to achieve. While he is still moving toward adult independence and may struggle to achieve longer separations from parents (e.g., sleep-away camp, trips alone to visit extended family), for the most part, this stage is all about feeling that "I can do it." Children who experience significant learning issues and frustration during this stage often need special work with their parents and teachers to help them develop a positive risk-taking style.

The 6- to 10-year-old also tolerates increased periods of frustration that leads to increased self-control. For example, the impulsive child who learns not to shout out in class but instead waits patiently to be called upon by the teacher is developing positive self-control that tempers positive risk-taking. In the social milieu the child forges ahead to risk making closer friendships and learns to survive and navigate the inevitable rejections of childhood. As the child develops intellectually, she begins to risk asserting her opinions, ideas, and beliefs, thereby chancing disapproval from her peer, teachers, or family.

LEARNING STYLE AND RISK-TAKING

Thanks to research in education, child development, and neuroscience we know far more about the components of the learning process than we did 50 years ago (Kanfer, Ackerman, & Cudeck, 1989; Levine, 1999, 2002, 2005; Vail, 1987). We can now appreciate the differences in the ways children learn, and we know better how to support their unique strengths and weaknesses. Often, despite helpful attempts by teachers and parents, there are many learning-disabled children who still end up feeling deflated or incompetent. Many children we have seen in our practices tend to feel stupid and unworthy, and they often begin to take poor risks (for example, clowning around in class) or take few good risks (for example, speaking up in class).

We have found over the years that the emergence of a child's learning difficulties can put a screeching halt to good risk-taking. This is because parents and children alike are sad, frustrated, and disappointed that they have (or must cope with) these challenges. A parent recently lamented, "My son used to be so happy, so outgoing. Now that he is struggling in school, everything seems to have changed for him." While learning good risk-taking isn't a panacea, the good risk-taker can better tolerate the struggle.

There are a number of ways to encourage good risk-taking when you've discovered your child has a learning disability. We elaborate on these items in the subsections below the list.

1. Learn everything you can about learning disabilities.
2. Consult with professionals.
3. Talk with your child about her learning style.
4. Pay attention to your own responses and reactions to your child's approach to learning.
5. Pay attention to your child's strengths.
6. Continue to have fun with your child! (Try to) let go of the worry—at least from time to time!

Learn Everything You Can

Parents who have a child showing early indications of a learning disability are wise to educate themselves about learning disabilities. There is a lot of information on the Web that can guide parents. A few of these include The Center for Learning Differences (http://www.centerforlearningdifferences.org/), the All Kinds of Minds Web site (http://www.all kinds of minds.org/), and the Learning Resource Network at the Jewish Board for Family and Children's Services (http://jbfcs.org/main/thinkingchildren.html). Just knowing about the causes, the diagnoses, and the treatment options can help ease the pain of the disability. Taking the step (the risk) to learn about learning issues also models proactive behavior for your child. Psychologist Howard Gardner (1993, 1999, 2006) expanded the traditional notions of intelligence in conceptualizing it as comprising several separate and different types of abilities, or "intelligences." A few of these include linguistic, logical, mathematical, interpersonal, and musical intelligences. Daniel Goleman's work elaborated upon Gardner's as he focused specifically on the development of emotional intelligence (Goleman, 1997, 2006). These two psychologists have widened our understanding of aptitude to include many strengths and traits that were previously not recognized or appreciated as facets of intelligence.

Consult with Professionals

Your child's teacher or pediatrician can direct you toward educational tutors, psychologists, and other specialists who can help you and your child address learning issues. Sometimes just taking the step toward recognizing your child's learning style goes a long way toward building or rebuilding his confidence about learning.

Talk Openly with Your Child

Speaking openly and comfortably to your child and others regarding his learning style is very important. Parents often ask, "When can I begin addressing these issues with my child?" It is never too early to talk about your child's strengths and weaknesses in a nonjudgmental, noncritical way—even if she's only 3 years old. As parents, it is usually better for us to listen more than we speak and to respond more than we offer advice.

Practice Self-Reflection

It is important to pay close attention to our own reactions as parents. (We will be discussing this topic in depth in Chapter 3.) A learning disability or other developmental difficulty can be upsetting for parents. They have so many wishes and dreams for their children, and they don't want them to experience frustration or difficulty. Therefore, parents can unwittingly transmit their own fears and reactions—frustration, disappointment, sadness, and worry—to their children and unintentionally make the situation worse for them. Again, keeping a diary of your thoughts, fears, and feelings, can be helpful.

Nurture Your Child's Strengths

Emphasize your child's abilities in other areas, such as sports, social interactions, music and art, and even household chores. Encourage him to take risks in these domains.

Enjoy Good Times with Your Child

Often the diagnosis of a learning disability is so devastating to a family that even the most optimistic parent begins to look at life's glass as half full. Continue to play and laugh with your child and look at all your child can do—and can do well.

KATIE AND DYLAN'S STORY

When Dylan entered preschool he was reticent to talk and play. Remember that Katie was worried about Dylan's development, particularly his language, which was slow to emerge. Dylan's temperament and his mom's sensitivity and family history exacerbated Dylan's issues at school and made him even more tongue-tied at school. Katie made the mistake of talking for Dylan, thus giving him the message that he was not able to speak for himself. Through his teachers' gentle talk with Katie, advice on how Katie could best help Dylan get involved and feel comfortable at school, and Katie's own self-reflection, things began to change for the better. Dylan took the risks involved in separating, made friends, and made strides both socially and intellectually. Over the next months and years in preschool Dylan's language skills kicked in, and his peers began to gravitate to him for his wit and gentle manner. Dylan had playdates at his house and those of his friends and had a successful experience in preschool.

When it came time for kindergarten, Dylan was ready to take the necessary risks involved in the transition. He was more confident and separated from his mom in a timely manner. As academics entered into the picture in first grade, Dylan was once again challenged, but this time the challenge was acquiring basic phonics skills. Math came fairly easily to him, but reading and reading comprehension were difficult. Again, Dylan began to shy away from risk-taking in the classroom. He had a lot of friends, but reading and speaking up in class was a problem. Initially, his teachers thought that his avoidance of homework and participation in class was a sign of opposition, and this misunderstanding caused them to criticize Dylan and his work. Katie was upset by her midyear school conference with Dylan's first-grade teacher and felt that Dylan was not properly understood. However, she too was frustrated by his forgetting to do homework. Katie wrote in her journal, "That first conference with Dylan's new teacher made me angry. She doesn't get Dylan. She treats him as if he were being bad, rather than just shy and slow to warm up. But to be honest, I'm getting frustrated with his pretending he doesn't have any homework."

Katie decided to get an objective opinion and consulted with the school psychologist. The psychologist recommended that Dylan undergo a learning evaluation at either the school's learning center or a local clinic to examine his learning strengths and weaknesses, so that they could better help him. Initially, Katie was overwhelmed by the seeming enormity of this recommendation, and wrote in her journal: "A learning evaluation! I hope Dylan doesn't have a big problem."

After investigating the cost of the testing, Katie decided to have Dylan evaluated by an educational psychologist within the local school system. The evaluation entailed two sessions, wherein the psychologist looked at Dylan's intellectual abilities, his reading and math skills, and his memory and information-processing skills. She found that Dylan had particular areas of strength—for example, in visual processing and abstract reasoning—but had some learning delays in language processing (no big surprise) that made the acquisition of phonics skills difficult for him. It was recommended that he work with a teacher one-on-one after school so that he could be taught a method of reading that was specifically suited to his cognitive strengths and weaknesses.

When Katie thought about her own experiences as a girl in school, she remembered her own tendency to shut down and become withdrawn when frustrated. She thought about how it must feel for Dylan to be struggling to learn to read and to have his teacher and mother frustrated with him. So Katie began to look at Dylan's challenges in a different light. Instead of becoming annoyed with him when he avoided homework, she empathized with his frustration and found ways to help Dylan approach his homework for shorter intervals, giving encouragement when he put attention and energy into it. She talked to him about the importance of making mistakes, because mistakes help people learn and told him stories about her own mistakes.

Katie scheduled another meeting with Dylan's teacher, and in advance of the meeting Katie gave her the test results to read. This time Katie was better able to comfortably advocate for her son. From the test report and Katie's new attitude, the teacher's perspective on Dylan shifted, and she too became more of a support to him in class. Through the help of tutoring and the phonics skills it built and through the attitude changes of his mother and teacher, Dylan slowly became a stronger reader and a risk-taker. Dylan was still relatively quiet in class; however, he was now on the trajectory toward taking more positive risks and tolerating his mistakes.

MORE OF LIFE'S BUMPS AND RISK-TAKING: DIVORCE, ILLNESS, AND LOSS

The diagnosis of a learning disability is only one of the many bumps a child may encounter in his life. When things don't go as planned—if a child experiences the illness of a family member, if his family makes a move to a new town and school, or if his parents divorce—the course of the child's risk-taking style can be altered. Like the diagnosis of a

---

FIGURE 2.1. Good Risk-Taking Despite Life's Bumps

- Educate yourself. Consult with your local librarian for book references, use Internet resources, and attend lectures and workshops on the topic.
- Consult with professionals about your own and your child's situation.
- Talk honestly and openly with your child—even a very young child—about the issue. In general, less is more. Listen more than you give advice or opinion.
- Pay attention to your own responses and reactions—frustration, disappointment, sadness, or worry. Monitor how your reactions impinge upon your child's functioning.
- Pay attention to your child's strengths. Your strengths and your child's strengths will get you through the worst of times.
- Let go of the worry and sadness at least occasionally. Find some time to have fun with your child. This is good medicine for all!

---

learning disability, these factors often significantly shift a child's usual risk-taking style. For example, a 10-year-old girl who was generally taking good risks in school, at home, and with friends may begin to take poor risks after her mother's battle with cancer. In a similar way, a 6-year-old boy who has lived through 2 years of constant fighting between his parents and a contentious divorce may demonstrate poor risk-taking. As with a learning disability, this trend is not irreversible. Using the same six principles discussed under "Learning Styles and Risk-Taking" above, parents can help their child move forward despite life's adversity. These principles are put in more inclusive terms outlined in Figure 2.1.

Risk-taking unfolds predictably with development, and sometimes, as parents, our job is to be active observers. At other times, steering our children toward a positive risk-taking style requires that we use the power that comes with understanding our children and understanding ourselves.

Chapter 3

THE PARENT'S PART: SELF-REFLECTION AND THE PRACTICE OF LISTENING

We do not believe in ourselves until someone reveals that deep inside us something is valuable, worth listening to, worthy of our trust, sacred to our touch. Once we believe in ourselves we can risk curiosity, wonder, spontaneous delight or any experience that reveals the human spirit.

—e.e. cummings

The ongoing parent-child relationship is an important context in which a child develops his risk-taking style. This is a mutual process—daily interactions between parent and child shape the kind of risk-taker the child becomes. As parents, we have the ability to influence and guide the ways in which our child approaches risks. Once parents have acquired a basic understanding of how risk-taking unfolds with child development, we are prepared to begin a two-part process of personal self-reflection and learning to listen to our children. The process of self-reflection helps us to see ourselves honestly, with all of our lumps and bumps, strengths and faults. After becoming more self-insightful, we are prepared to see our children for who they are, rather than as an extension of who we would like them to be. Through listening carefully to our children, we can help them become good risk-takers. Careful listening involves hearing what our children say and what they don't say; it also involves careful observation of our children. We need to pay attention to how they look when they are talking to us: their facial expressions, body language, and demeanor. This chapter explains we explain how learning these skills of self-reflection and communication impact directly the ways in which children take risks.

THE PROCESS OF SELF-REFLECTION

The parent-child relationship is an intensely loving, yet challenging, human relationship. As parents, we are faced with the great task of rearing our child from infancy through adulthood. It can be a daunting job to care for our new infant, whose every moment of survival depends mainly on us. When a newborn comes into the world, we are humbled by the extent to which our child is dependent on us. Many a parent has developed a wholly different approach to the world, defined by the need to protect the baby. Mothers particularly talk about how they have become light sleepers and can be awakened from a dead slumber by their child's faint cries from the next room.

Even as our child develops and grows toward independence, we continue to be entangled in the spectacular, at times overwhelming, and always complicated web of relationship between us. As parents, we know that our children from early on have an uncanny knack for zeroing in on who we really are—hypocrisies, biases, and all. They often force us to come face-to-face with the undeveloped or hidden parts of ourselves. For example, how can we avoid looking at our behavior when our 5-year-old asks, "How come you scream so loud, Mommy, when stuff spills on our carpet?" It is our children's questions that might compel us to begin to look deeply inside ourselves. The ultimate gift of becoming more self-reflective is that not only are we better able to understand our children, but we can also better realize our impact upon our family, friends, and colleagues.

So, how do we self-reflect? Learning to self-reflect is a worthwhile part of everyday life and can become a natural and automatic skill. To become a more self-reflective parent, we must begin to ask ourselves some basic questions such as, "What is it about me—my history and my style—that causes me to react in certain ways with my child?" This process is not meant to be judgmental or self-critical. In fact, we can sabotage this process if we are too harsh with ourselves. We are merely collecting data, so to speak, about who we are as parents. We are noticing our parenting style and how it has evolved.

Self-Reflection Can Ruffle Our Feathers

As parents self-reflect we may become aware, for example, that we speak rather sternly and uncomfortably, or shut down and become silent, when the topic of sex and sexuality arises. In this process we need to be honest, even if it ruffles our feathers or shakes up our self-concept. Maybe we're not always the easygoing hipster we thought we were, or maybe we have more inhibitions about sexuality than we thought. We need to trust ourselves, which is not an easy thing. In Benjamin Spock's (1946) words, "Trust yourself, you know more than you think you do."

Through practice we have found that it is most effective to begin with the immediate here-and-now and then gradually delve into the past influences on our behavior. Therefore, we have devised three parent checklists to help parents develop greater self-awareness. (See Figures 3.1, 3.2, and 3.3).

Judy and Hannah's Story

An anecdote about Judy and Hannah can be helpful for understanding these concepts. Judy gave birth to Hannah when she had already been teaching kindergarten for several years. Judy noticed in her classes that when a child was cautious and timid about playing in the playground, there was often an overly vigilant and fearful parent at home. Judy's own parents had sheltered her. So she felt that she understood this cycle. She would counsel parents to be mindful of how their anxiety was being expressed to their children, and suggest ways for them to support their child's physical development and the need for rigorous, playful outdoor time.

When Hannah emerged in her toddler and preschool years as a highly active, spontaneous, and somewhat impulsive child, Judy was put to the test. Although she had helped other parents, her own anxieties were another story! As Hannah swung from the highest bar of the jungle gym, Judy's heart was in her throat. She found herself running over to the jungle gym, admonishing her daughter for climbing so high, yelling, "You're too high. That's too dangerous!" At first, Hannah would laugh and climb further away from Judy. As she did so, Judy's anxiety increased, and she began to warn Hannah at the beginning of every playground excursion, "You better not climb too high!" It was not only the words Judy used, but also her tone of voice and demeanor that communicated Judy's anxiety to Hannah. Judy's overreaction gave Hannah an inflated sense of power, and she began to take even more dangerous risks to get a rise out of her mother. For example, Hannah would run out of sight and hide, then tease, "Here I am, Mom," as she mischievously emerged from a hiding place after Judy had been searching frantically for her.

Judy's friend, also a teacher, accompanied Judy and Hannah to the playground one day. She had her slightly older child in tow. The friend picked up on Judy's tense and heightened emotions and the way she chastised Hannah when she ran fast or climbed high. She commented to Judy, "If I can feel your anxiety, imagine how Hannah's feeling about it. Hannah needs your limits, but you know better than anyone else how this is not an effective way to get her to be more careful." Upon hearing her friend's remarks, Judy was initially hurt and angry. She felt criticized and said, "I happen to have a highly active young child who was doing dangerous things!"

Upon reflection, Judy decided (reluctantly) that her friend had a point, that she was acting out parts of her own childhood that she had over time internalized. Judy began to see herself as the overprotective

---

FIGURE 3.1: Self-Reflection Checklist—The Here and Now

- Is my child's behavior triggering uncomfortable feelings (e.g., anger, anxiety, fear, or sadness) in me at this moment? Describe these feelings.
- Why is this behavior/need of my child making me feel this way?
- Is this a familiar feeling for me or an unexpected feeling? Why?
- How is my reaction affecting my child's behavior?
- How is my reaction affecting my behavior?

---

parent who was not giving her child enough room to explore and take risks. This was upsetting to Judy because she had prided herself on her knowledge of child development and her capacity to know herself well. She wrote in her journal, "What an eye-opener I had today at the playground. My friend basically told me that I'm a worrywart just like someone else I know well—*my mom!*"

After some soul-searching, frequent talks with her friend, and making notes in her journal about her interactions with Hannah in risky situations, Judy was able to learn more about herself. She also increased her understanding of Hannah in the process. As Judy learned to understand her anxiety in response to her daughter's physical risk-taking, she was somewhat better able to manage her feelings and allow Hannah a healthier amount of freedom. She was also able to talk to Hannah in a more authoritative tone (nurturing, yet setting firm rules, as opposed to authoritarian or rigid and controlling) to set limits when her child's physical risks were too extreme.

How to Begin

Figure 3.1 lists some questions parents can pose to begin the process of self-reflection when faced with a current problematic situation with their child. These questions, that can be mulled over alone, with a friend, or with a partner or spouse, provide a guide for beginning this process. We recommend that you note your answers and examples in your ongoing journal.

For Judy, her friend brought this problem to her attention, but there are many other occasions that could have red-flagged her overprotective behavior and forced her to confront it. Perhaps Hannah's teacher might have addressed Hannah's tendency to ignore adult warnings about safety and asked Judy how this issue was being handled at home. Or maybe Judy's overprotective behavior might have gone unchecked for a longer period of time, creating more ingrained oppositional behavior for Hannah. Or perhaps an accident might have occurred, forcing Judy to self-reflect on her contribution to Hannah's poor risk-taking behavior.

Discovering Family of Origin

Once Judy began the process of self-reflection, she realized that she clearly had uncomfortable feelings and sometimes all-out fear when Hannah took physical risks. She was surprised, at first, that her history of her mother's anxiety about physical safety was affecting her behavior with Hannah. She thought that she had already confronted these issues as a young adult. For example, in her early 20s, she went on a ski trip with her boyfriend and came face-to-face with her paralyzing anxiety. She self-reflected on her fears and began to unravel her childhood memories of physical activity. Her worries about safety issues arose again when she was in graduate school studying child development and began to work with children as a teacher. But, as we've learned, old issues can return again at new stages of our life—especially when we become parents.

Through self-reflection, Judy was able to understand how her parents' behavior shaped her own parenting approach with Hannah. This intergenerational transmission of conscious and unconscious thoughts and behaviors was brought into her awareness and thoughtfully considered.

Even if we believe that as parents we are making conscious decisions about the way our parents raised us, we can unthinkingly make similar mistakes with our own children. For example, studies concur that children who were abused physically have a far greater chance of using corporal punishment with their children (Wekerle & Wolfe, 2002). Abuse and criticism, tolerance and nurturance, all become internalized by children and are passed down to the next generation.

After you've started answering the questions in Figure 3.1, ask yourself the questions about your family of origin, which are posed in Figure 3.2. This part of the process will help you understand more deeply the origin of your parenting style.

FIGURE 3.2. Self-Reflection Checklist—Family of Origin

- What was your childhood like? Be specific. Think about some happy memories. Think also of some sad or angry ones.
- What was your relationship with your parent(s) like? What was it about your parent(s) that made you feel safe or insecure, happy or sad, calm or anxious, accepted or rejected?
- What was your parents' style when you were growing up? Were your parents' styles similar or different? How so? For blended families, how did your stepparent's style make you feel?
- Were your parent(s) kind and generous?
- Were they harsh and punitive?
- Were your parent(s) shy and withdrawn, or were they social and gregarious?
- How did you feel about your parent(s)? Were you often proud of them? Or did you often feel ashamed and humiliated by their actions and behaviors?
- Are your reactions toward your own child similar or different from the way your own parent(s) reacted when you acted this way?
- How did your parents react to the risks that you took or needed to take? Were they anxious and fearful, supportive or authoritative? How did they handle the positive and the negative risks?

More Questions to Ask Ourselves

Asking yourself about your upbringing often brings more questions. You begin to understand that there are many factors that can impinge upon your parenting style toward raising good risk-takers. Figure 3.3 is an extensive checklist for parents to use after they have thought through many of the issues listed in the first two checklists. Figure 3.3 contains seven sections designed to elicit more thorough examination of how you were parented. This checklist asks questions about how a number of issues were handled in your family of origin, including:

- How were feelings or emotional reactions managed or avoided?
- How were transitions and separations handled?
- How was limit setting and boundary setting approached?
- How were strong feelings managed?

FIGURE 3.3. Self-Reflection Checklist—Advanced Topics

The Role of Feelings in the Family

- Could your parents talk about difficult or intense feelings such as anger, sadness or joy? Or did they tend to avoid these conversations?
- Did they encourage you to express your feelings?
- Did you feel uncomfortable—or even humiliated—if you expressed vulnerable feelings?

Transitions and Separations

- What was your experience with separations when you were a child?
- Did you cry a lot when your parents left you at preschool or day care?
- How did your parents react? Were they comforting and understanding, or did they seem humiliated or annoyed at your behavior?
- Do you remember if your parents seemed anxious about the separation—checking back time and again—even when you were playing happily?
- Did you have a difficult time leaving to go on overnights with friends?
- Did your parents seem to have a hard time without you? How did they show this?

Limits and Boundaries

- How hands-on were your parents? In what ways did you feel that they were intrusive? For example, did they listen in on phone conversations or look at personal diaries without your consent? Did they open a closed door without knocking?
- Did you feel that your parents were unavailable to you? Do you wish that they had taken more of an interest in your activities and interests?

How Parents Regulated Strong Feelings

- During arguments or times of stress or crisis how did your parent(s) react? Did you observe them going from calm to angry/frightened/hysterical rapidly? How did you feel about their reactions?
- Or did your parent(s) disconnect themselves emotionally from you and other members of the family when they were stressed or in crisis?
- Could they easily regain emotional equilibrium or did strong feelings set off a series of outbursts?
- How did your parent(s) react to your emotional ups and downs? Did your feelings frighten them?
- Did you feel that your parents could tolerate, manage, and contain your (and their) emotional patterns?

FIGURE 3.3. Continued

Discipline

- Did your parents tend to be pushovers, strict but fair, or harsh in the way in which they enforced rules and discipline? Did they react consistently or erratically?
- Were there lots of explicit rules, or were there few rules?
- How were these rules enforced? With consistency? Were they fairly enforced?
- What happened if you disobeyed a rule?

Achievement and Mastery

- How did your parents react to your achievements and setbacks? Were they supportive or competitive with achievements; critical or tolerant and soothing with failures? Did you sometimes feel that they were overly positive—praising you about every little achievement and not allowing you to experience these daily ups, or downs, yourself?
- Did your parents model tenacity and going for the challenge, or did they retreat when things got tough. How did they cope with their own failures or applaud their achievements?

Sexuality and Sexual Development

- Was sex and sexual development talked about easily and informatively? Was sex a taboo subject?
- Did your parents talk to you about sexuality and sexual development? How old were you when they spoke with you about these issues? What do you remember about these talks together?
- During adolescence, were you comfortable about your sexuality? How did your sexual behavior in young adulthood reflect your parents' comfort (or discomfort) with sexuality?

- How was discipline approached and managed?
- How were issues about mastery and achievement taught?
- How were issues of sexuality discussed—or avoided?

Parents can begin this part of the process by thinking about the ways in which feelings were managed in their family of origin. We can also think about the ways in which transitions and separations were handled by our parents, and how our parents were, or were not, able to help us manage our intense emotions. In the psychology literature this is called *affect regulation*, or the ability to have intense feelings and either express them, control them, or redirect them, depending on the appropriateness of the situation.

Since part of a parent's role is to help a child approach achievement and mastery effectively but without undo pressure, it is also helpful to think about the ways in which our parents handled these issues. For example, in Louis's family of origin he was expected to achieve. His parents worked hard and wanted a better life for their children, so they held them to very strict standards and high expectations. Anything less was met with their obvious disappointment.

Finally, it is critical to reflect specifically upon how our parents talked about—or avoided—sexuality and sexual development, since our child's risk-taking style will strongly influence how she approaches sexuality when she is an adolescent. Connecting intimately with another human being can be an enormous risk and can comprise, at times, any or all of life's universal risks.

How Katie Used This Checklist

After Katie had spent some time using the first two checklists, she began to wonder about the ways in which sad and angry feelings were avoided in her family of origin. She grew up not knowing quite how to articulate and express feelings (although she felt them deeply) because negative emotions were so discouraged by her parents. In her diary Katie wrote, "When I was a kid if I had a freak-out, my parents would say, 'Now, now dear, there is no need for that sort of thing. In our family we just grin and bear it when things get tough.' Until Dylan was born, I didn't know how this sort of talk affected me." In her self-reflection, Katie also came to appreciate that her parents had clear boundaries and were respectful of her privacy. They were not intrusive into her friendships and her social life: "The fact that my parents trusted me, and were respectful of my friendships makes all of this so much easier with my own kids," she wrote.

These snippets from Katie's diary were part of her ongoing work in which she examined the intergenerational transmission of feelings. This work began when Dylan started preschool at age 3 ½. He had just begun to form sentences and verbally assert his likes, dislikes, requests, and feelings. However, he only felt comfortable speaking at home among his family members. When around other people, he was quiet.

Katie remembered how the initial weeks of separation at preschool were very difficult for both of them. She also remembered how she had hovered closely watching Dylan's interactions with his classmates and listening to his conversations. At times, she even remembered that she would talk for him to facilitate his making friends. She had so wanted Dylan to become a successful member of the class and to learn to make friends. Katie remembered vividly how Dylan had felt her surveillance, had reacted by retreating back to her lap, and how her anxiety had actually made matters worse for him.

Katie remembered how helpful Dylan's teacher had been. She had called Katie at home to suggest that she take a step back and trust Dylan to find his own way into the class activity. She said that it is the teacher's role to help him feel safe and venture forth. As uncomfortable as this was for Katie, it is what Dylan needed from her.

Katie initially wrote in her diary, "Dylan's teacher said that *she* will help Dylan feel safe in school. Who does she think she is? I'm his mother and I'm the one that makes him feel safe."

Eventually Katie realized that "she had her back up" and was threatened by the teacher's authoritative role. This prompted more self-reflection about how Katie's parents had hovered over her. She was taught to play it safe and was encouraged as a child to avoid risks that could potentially lead to failure.

She also realized that although she was a budding artist and photographer, her parents discouraged her spending too much time on artistic pursuits and instead encouraged focus on school and social activities with friends—being "happy and popular" was the way to go. Katie, however, didn't feel bubbly and popular. She remembered feeling angry at her parents for misunderstanding her. Yet she didn't articulate these feelings, and instead complied with their requests. She stayed away from risks and ended up in the field of corporate human resources. Because she was an artist at heart, she found her job tedious and ungratifying. She eventually became aware of how her own fears held her back in life. She began to make plans about stepping out, spending more time on her art, and ultimately looking for a gallery to show her work.

Dylan's first weeks at preschool coincided with the beginning of this earnest self-reflection. Dylan's discomfort in school led her to mull over some big questions for herself. She thought about her childhood and what it was like. She thought of happy memories, and some sad and angry ones. She thought about her relationship with her parents and how she felt secure and loved in some respects, but did not feel accepted for the whole of who she was—the unusual, creative artist in her felt rejected.

Katie also thought about the way that feelings were dealt with in her family. In her family they spoke a lot at the dinner table about the events of the day and how school was going, but not about feelings that had any intensity to them. Anything that felt uncomfortable was discouraged from conversation, so Katie learned to keep difficult and strong feelings to herself. On the rare occasion that she would "lose it," her parents would chastise her.

Katie also thought about how separations were handled in her family. Katie had difficulty separating from her mother in nursery school and kindergarten, and cried inconsolably in class, on and off for months. Katie began to realize, as she recollected these first days in kindergarten, that both her mother and she had difficulty separating, and that her mother's need to keep her so close reflected her mother's fears and anxieties that she had likely picked up. Now she was passing these fears on to her son.

Katie was wary of taking the risk of having Dylan separate, emotionally and physically. It certainly was a risk for her because of all the rational and irrational feelings of danger inherent in the close bond with her young child. The self-reflection was painful, but it helped her know herself and Dylan much better. This event early in Dylan's life and in Katie's life as a parent led to changes in Katie's behavior and, consequently, changes in Dylan's behavior. This mix of self-insight and careful attention to emotion and behavior makes us more empathic and intuitive parents.

THE PRACTICE OF LISTENING

A parent who is equipped with greater self-insight and who is more attuned to her child after engaging in the process of self-reflection is ready to begin the practice of listening. Listening, like other skills, takes time, patience and practice. Good listening fosters good risk-taking because we become attuned and more precise sounding boards for our children. Renowned psychoanalyst and author Chaim Ginott (1965) wrote, "The beginning of wisdom is listening" (p. 198). Effective listening is an active process that involves focusing on one person to the relative exclusion of other people and things. It includes being able to step out of one's own internal thoughts, which can interfere with attending to what the other person is saying and how he says it. It means paying attention to content as well as voice intonation, volume, and other vocal characteristics. Body language is also important; how a person expresses himself by his body posture, body tension, or relaxation is integrally related to the meaning of the words he uses. Listening for what a person leaves out is also essential: What someone says and also what he doesn't say lets us know how he's feeling.

LOUIS AND CHRIS'S STORY

When Chris was 4 years old, Louis enrolled him in a sports class at the local Y. It was a class in which parents participated with their children. Louis loved spending this active time with his son helping him develop the skills that he would need to become a good athlete. The mothers and fathers would encourage their children to jump and roll, throw, catch, and run in response to the teacher's instructions. Chris was developing normally; however, he was not quite ready for all of the activities. He had difficulty catching the oversized ball that some of the other children did with ease. Louis wanted Chris to be an athletic child, and he worked overtime with Chris on catching and throwing, despite Chris's clear lack of readiness for this particular skill.

"Catch it, Chris," Louis would shout. "No—not like that. C'mon—what's wrong with you?"

Chris reacted to Louis's insistence by running away from his father during catching and throwing time. Louis didn't get the message that his son was communicating. Through his emotions and behaviors, Chris was telling his father that catching and throwing were not fun for him. Instead of listening to his child's communication, Louis kept pushing Chris to learn the skills. Although Chris was not saying it in words, his actions were telling his father to lay off.

Why couldn't Louis understand what Chris was telling him, and why was he not able to listen well? He listened perfectly well when his boss and coworkers spoke to him, but not to his son, particularly when it came to sports. Louis had his own agenda, and that was overriding his ability to listen well to his son.

It was Louis's wife, Liz, who brought his poor listening skills to his attention. Louis was complaining to Liz that Chris wasn't trying hard enough, as he was working with him on his motor skills. Liz recognized this tendency of Louis's to not listen, because it happened with her as well. She reminded her husband that their son was only 4, and told him that Chris was not the one with the problem—he was. She also said, in no uncertain terms, that it was understandable that Chris was getting upset and running away from him in class. Instead of forcing Chris to do something that he's not ready for, why not find something else that would be fun to do with the ball, like kicking it? The point was to have fun while developing skills. The more Chris had fun in the class, the more he'd gravitate to athletics and want to improve his skills.

Louis had some trouble hearing this advice from his wife. He was angry with her and Chris. He had always excelled at everything he did, and throughout his childhood he longed to have the leisure time for sports. Chris's lack of gross–motor readiness upset him; he needed to have a child who, like him, excelled. Liz reasoned with Louis that Chris is a different child, and being a good parent means figuring out what's best for Chris, not Louis. This figurative "kick in the backside" woke Louis up to his role in the problem.

Louis thought back to his own childhood and remembered how different everything was for him. He thought about how angry he was about his own childhood, especially about having two parents who had little time for him. With Liz's help, Louis considered Chris's needs more and began to learn how to listen.

In this scenario, listening entailed first becoming aware of the intensity of his own need for his son to excel, then paying attention to Chris's behavior and avoidance of the activity. He learned that his needs and his son's needs were different entities and that as a good parent, he would have to go along with what his son needed. He had to pay close attention to Chris's behavior during the group class. Did he seem happy and engaged with the other children? In contrast, how did he behave when it was just the two of them practicing?

Over time Louis found that following Chris's lead was actually a lot more fun for both of them. Typically, they would happily kick the ball back and forth for a while, and then go and get some hot chocolate and talk. While Chris wasn't the strongest child in the league, Louis enjoyed the time getting to know his son better.

What Is This All About?

Listening to your child is an experience that can be enjoyable for both of you. It is a powerful process of attentiveness that communicates to your child how you feel about him. Through listening well, a parent is conveying the message that his child is compelling enough, clever enough, and lovable enough to deserve full and uninterrupted attention. By listening only half-heartedly—by glancing elsewhere, missing pieces of what he is saying, and running off to answer the ringing telephone—a parent is conveying a very different message.

As parents, we have hundreds of opportunities to listen to our children everyday, and every interaction doesn't have to be perfectly attuned. It is over the course of many years that a child learns that her parent understands and listens to her. Of course, parents cannot be emotionally present all of the time, nor should we be. Being a parent means having worries and responsibilities, and we cannot be fully available to our children whenever or wherever they need us.

Realistically, these everyday limitations on our time and attention challenge a growing child's frustration tolerance, and this is an important life lesson for them. As debilitating as life can be for a child whose parents do not have the time or capacity to listen, parents who micromanage every aspect of their child's life is giving their child the message that she is incapable of achieving independently. Children with parents who are overly preoccupied with their every step grow up to wonder if they are really worthy of all of the fuss. These children often end up struggling to find pleasure in their own accomplishments. This is an essential part of self-esteem and confidence.

D. W. Winnicott (1975), the British pediatrician and psychoanalyst who created the concept of "good-enough mothering," suggested that parents must find some balance over time in meeting their child's needs. This needs to be done in a way in which the child feels loved and supported and special, but has the capacity to tolerate frustration when things don't go well and to be able to soothe himself when feeling bad. A parent who has done the work of self-reflection and has learned to listen well is better able to know how to soothe himself and his child. This enables the child to develop this capacity for himself.

The "good-enough" parent who listens well and does the work of self-reflection enables his child to become emotionally expressive and to feel secure and balanced. Active listening, which entails hearing what our child truly needs from us at that moment, is a crucial part of good-enough parenting. We learn about what's on our child's mind, for example, how the day went, the way she is feeling about her school work, and her interactions with friends. If we give these mundane, everyday events cursory attention, we risk missing subtle yet important feelings or thoughts that are brewing, but not yet articulated by our child.

The better we listen, the better we know our children. We become more equipped to help them manage the vicissitudes of growing up. Good listening, though, is not to be confused with micromanaging our children's affairs or scrutinizing them. We need to learn how to subtly pick up the signals that tell us when a child is upset or has experienced something confusing or troubling. A mother of five children who has practiced the skill of good listening said that she could tell what kind of day any of her children had as soon as the child emerged from the school building 100 feet away. Without a spoken word exchanged between them, she understood how her child was feeling from the cues in her walk (buoyant or downbeat), facial expression (animated or sad), and eye gaze (sparkling or downcast).

Of course, listening well is easier with some children than with others. Some children tend to hold feelings in or are secretive in ways that others are not. Some children wear their emotions on their sleeves and yet cannot quite articulate what is really going on inside. Still others seem to be intuitively aware and able to articulate their feelings and, with hardly any prompting, can share thoughts and feelings readily. Every child has his unique way of experiencing and expressing feelings. With some children we need to work harder and listen to them in a deeper way in order to know what's going on; we need to actively provide them with the opportunity to talk. We need to keep our antennae tuned for that moment when they are ready to talk. It can happen during a television commercial break or on the way to the school bus stop. It is up to us as parents to respond to our children's cues.

Listening to Build Intimacy and Empathy

In listening well to our child, we communicate a level of intimacy that makes her feel connected to us, while it teaches her the building blocks to enjoy other intimate relationships in life. By actively and sensitively listening to our child, we convey an emotional presence and a sense of empathy that can be even more powerful than physical touch. The child learns that when her parent is with her in the truest sense, she is not alone with her feelings. She develops the inner strength to manage and tolerate feelings of all kinds. Children also learn that others can be close with us, and us with them, and that this emotional intimacy is comfortable and natural. We know that we are on our way toward communicating these values to our children when our child tells us, "Mom, I had an awful day at school," and he proceeds to talk about it. Or when she says," I really missed you when I was staying at Grandma's house. But then I thought about what you'd say, just how you'd make me feel."

Empathy is an essential part of good listening. Being empathic means that we are imagining ourselves in someone else's predicament; we feel another's feelings. We extend past our own feelings and circumstances to try to know what an experience feels like from another's perspective. It is a profound gesture of understanding and generosity because it can be painful to know the sadness or pain of another. In some cases when we listen with empathy, we do so with some modicum of distance, and at other times we come much closer and feel deeply as we listen. The situation usually dictates what is required. If, for example, a child cries crocodile tears in an attempt to manipulate attention, an empathic response is not appropriate or helpful. When feelings are truly hurt, or a child is worried or in pain, soothing and empathic concern are what is needed. Through repeated experiences with a parent who is an empathic listener, our children become empathic themselves.

When a 7-year-old says, "I feel so sad for that homeless man on the street. Do you think we can buy him some dinner?" chances are this child has already had repeated experiences in which his own feelings—sad, angry, fearful, and joyful—have been heard by his parents. When a 6-year-old asks her mother if grandma is lonely living by herself after grandpa died, we know that this child is exercising the basic skills of empathy.

Sometimes our child may need to talk about some feelings, or just express emotions through weeping or even silence, and we are required to say very little. This can be extremely challenging for those who are used to always doing something actively and have the tendency to want to "fix" everything. Simply acknowledging our children's feelings, and literally sitting with them, aware of what they're feeling at the moment, is sometimes exactly what is required. This type of listening is communicating that whether or not we are completely aware of how they are feeling at the moment, we are able to help them tolerate these feelings until they can work them out alone or with some help. (Again, having done the work of self-reflection helps us, as parents, to better tolerate these feelings in ourselves.) Listening doesn't always entail speaking. A child may be proud of an accomplishment and may not be ready to talk about it. Perhaps this child needs, for a variety of reasons, to keep this accomplishment and the feelings that go along with it to himself. In listening fully, a parent must be able to tolerate whatever the child will, or will not, bring up. As parents, we can often become too zealous in complimenting our children. Like the child who is micromanaged, the child whose parent lauds every drawing as a masterpiece is doing his child a disservice.

However, if a child consistently hides his success or shies away from achieving it, a parent must think about possible reasons for this pattern and perhaps plan some interventions. It could be that the child is afraid of upstaging a vulnerable family member, or perhaps the child thinks his accomplishment will be devalued within the family or pale next to a highly successful sibling.

Katie and Jesse's Story

Dylan's difficult entry into preschool reverberated throughout the family. At this time, Katie's older son, Jesse, was 5 and beginning to read. Katie noticed that Jesse was downplaying his achievements. Jesse was pretending that he wasn't yet able to string together the basic sentences in the children's books he would pore over for long periods of time. Katie found out from Jesse's teacher that he was, in fact, reading Dr. Seuss books on his own. Katie wondered why Jesse hadn't let her in on his exciting leap forward, but she also realized that Jesse was picking up on her worry and preoccupation over Dylan's beginning months at preschool. Katie asked Jesse about why he didn't share with her his exciting news. Jesse told her that he felt sad that Dylan "wasn't making friends at school" and he "didn't want Dylan to feel bad because he was happy." Then Katie understood that her older son was more sensitive than she had previously thought and was already showing signs of developed empathy skills. Yet she also knew that Jesse's holding back was not good for him.

Katie told Jesse, "Your concern for your brother is a very loving thing, but you need to feel proud of yourself for your accomplishments and feel happy about the good things in your life." She assured Jesse that his accomplishments would not make Dylan feel less about himself.

That night Katie wrote in her journal, "I just assumed that Jesse let situations roll off him and that Dylan was the sensitive one. But it's not that simple. Each of my children are sensitive and vulnerable, but in different ways, and they are affected by things that go on in the family, even if it's not directly about them."

Listening Can Ruffle Our Feathers

As parents, we sometimes hear or learn things that can be upsetting or painful. Children might need to tell you how they misbehaved in school or treated someone cruelly. They may brag unappealingly about an accomplishment or a vindication, or indicate that something feels humiliating to them. We may not want to see or know these aspects of our children. As parents who have done the preliminary work of self-reflection, we are better equipped to listen to the feelings and motivations that our children have, and separate them from our own feelings and expectations for them.

JUDY AND HANNAH'S STORY

One day, Hannah came home from kindergarten announcing with loud bravado that she was the best "climber, runner, and soccer player in the whole class" and, with a disparaging tone, that her best friend, Chloe, was the "worst, worst, worst." She said that she and Chloe had gotten into an argument about it. When Judy inquired further and learned that Hannah had readily told Chloe just what she thought about their different abilities, Judy quickly and curtly told her that she was being mean to her friend and she should stop bragging. As the words left her mouth, her sharp tone surprised her, and caused her to reflect on why she had responded in such a way to Hannah. She thought about her own tendency to be humble and value such characteristics in others. She didn't find Hannah's self-aggrandizing to be an attractive trait, and in fact, she disliked it.

Judy decided to listen to Hannah's communication more clearly, trying to hear what she was saying, rather than what she thought she was saying. She wondered whether the lessons in school that focused on learning about letters, letter sounds, and introductory academics were making Hannah feel less able than the other children, since she was not yet able to sit for long periods and attend in class. She wondered whether Hannah was playing up her physical strengths in an attempt to feel more competent. Judy decided to ask Hannah's teacher how things were going in kindergarten. She made an appointment to see her after school and the teacher told Judy that, in fact, Hannah was not participating in circle time when letters and letter sounds were discussed. She added, "Hannah often looks uncomfortable and withdrawn when I call on her to give an answer."

Judy thought about this conversation with Hannah's teacher and the possible reasons for Hannah's bragging. This helped her understand Hannah better and be less quick to criticize. And Judy and Hannah's teacher continued to work together to encourage Hannah's comfort with oral expression in the classroom.

Listening Well Is Different from Accepting All of Our Child's Behaviors

Parents must be clear about teaching children right from wrong, and about setting clear limits and disciplinary actions. Mogel (2001) emphasizes the importance of kind and gentle but firm limit setting and disciplinary strategies. Learning to listen well does not negate the importance of determining these strategies.

If, for example, your daughter bullied another child or stole something, you would not listen to condone the behavior; instead, you would listen carefully to understand why she behaved as she did, and also to determine whether some specific disciplinary action would need to be taken to rectify the situation. Listening as calmly as possible to your child's misbehaviors is as important as listening to her accomplishments or her fears. This type of listening involves several specific steps: First, ask your child about the situation, and listen carefully to what she says; second, talk with her about what why she behaved in an unacceptable way; and third, decide on appropriate—and fair—consequences for the misbehavior.

LOUIS AND CHRIS'S STORY

Once, when Chris was in kindergarten, he took a book from his friend's bookshelf and stashed it in his backpack. Louis found the book and asked Chris about it. At first, Chris wouldn't admit that he had stolen the book. He told his father that his friend had given it to him. Louis was suspicious and replied that he needed to hear the truth, and that if he wasn't certain that Chris was telling the truth he would call his friend's parent and check it out. Then Chris admitted that he had taken it without permission.

"Why?" Louis asked. "I would have bought you that book if you had asked me."

"I don't know," Chris stammered. "I guess I was jealous that he had so many toys and books."

Louis had been practicing listening to his son: "I got how you feel, Chris. That's not the bad part. Feel whatever . . . . Still, you can't take what isn't yours." Louis told Chris that he had to give the book back to his friend and apologize for taking it. Chris was upset and said he would be embarrassed. However, his father insisted. The next day (with some difficulty) Chris gave back the book and apologized to his friend.

Understanding Problem Behaviors

It is essential that, no matter what intervention or punishment is taken, you help your child understand his motivations and feelings underlying the problem behavior. In Chris's situation, he had taken a bad risk (stealing the book from his friend) and through his conversation with his father and his father's strict, but fair, mandate, he was able to take a good, but difficult, risk that led him to apologize and return the book to his friend. To be sure, not every conversation nor intervention will result in a dramatic shift in your child's risk-taking behavior. It is only over time, and as we become increasingly adept at self-reflection and listening, that we can use these tools to develop the capacity to guide our children toward good risk-taking.

Issues often emerge when we have a newborn and a toddler at home. If, for example, your toddler says, "I hate my little sister and I want her to go back to the hospital," it means she is experiencing strong and overwhelming emotions about having a new competitor in the household. She feels, at the moment, that she would like things to be the same as they used to be. Feelings aren't always pretty and they aren't always comfortable. We need to model and teach our children to feel their feelings freely and to understand that behavior is quite separate from feelings. We may harbor some anger and annoyance toward our 3-year-old for her aggression toward the newborn, but by becoming aware of our own sentiments, we have the choice of how to act or not act on them.

Just Let Your Child Feel

If we realize that our child is angry and hurt at being displaced by a new baby, it might be sufficient to let her know that we understand that she has lots of different feelings about her new sibling (by having listened intently to her feelings) and that it is okay to use her words, but not her actions, to express these feelings. We may need to encourage her to talk about how she feels, anger and all, and ask her how she imagines the baby will change her life. Through the process of empathic listening, as well as reassurances of your love, your child will feel loved and understood. This goes a long way in making the feelings tolerable for her until they go away.

Parents are often unaware that they at times control what their child says by expressing negative, or positive, feelings in response to something the child said. If in the situation above you initially responded to your daughter's statement about her little sister with, "Don't say that, be a good girl," you're teaching her that she is "not good" if she shares angry thoughts and feelings. This is confusing feelings and thoughts with behavior. Banging the baby on the head is a behavior. Talking about hitting the baby on the head is not a behavior; it is a thought and/or fantasy. If your child talks to you about her anger, it is a good thing, because you can help her come to terms with these feelings and

---

FIGURE 3.4. Six Reasons Why the Practice of Listening Is Essential for Raising Good Risk-Takers

- Listening to our children is the best way to learn who are children are (temperamentally) and where they are at (developmentally). Listening effectively is better than any report that we get from a teacher, day-care worker, or babysitter.
- Listening well helps us see our children clearly, and thus we can value them for who they are. When our children know that they are accepted as valuable human beings by their parents, the foundation toward taking good risks is established.
- Listening well helps us see our children's strengths. If we focus on their weaknesses, their risk-taking behavior will follow suit.
- Listening to our children helps develop their self-confidence. Children who are more confident are better able to take good risks.
- Listening well can convey loving emotions as much as a hug. A look, a nod, a simple phrase such as, "That's okay, I am in your court anyway," can convey a strong emotional presence. Listening well, though, does not replace the need for a hug. Children grow best in an environment in which love and care are interchanged generously and genuinely.
- As an interactive experience, listening well facilitates having more fun with your children and enjoying who they are.

---

learn that the verbalization of that feeling is okay. It is the actual doing of it that is not okay, and would have very bad consequences for the baby, and also for the older child.

Parents are in a powerful position in which, from their child's birth onward, they are teaching their child about the complicated world of human interactions. Learning is based on connections between behaviors and responses, and we all influence our children by the ways—and times—we dole out affection, praise, rewards, and punishments. Sometimes our best intentions can communicate the opposite of what we want our children to learn. We must allow our child to have and to experience her own feelings, separate from ours.

Practicing Active Listening

In this chapter we have discussed how listening to our children is essential to parenting for good risk-taking. Good listening helps build a strong parent-child bond, and it is through this connection that a child's risk-taking style develops. Figure 3.4 summarizes why listening is essential.

FIGURE 3.5. A Parent's Listening Checklist

- Begin by an assessment of the current state of how you listen to your child. For example, when your child asks you a question or engages you in conversation, do you find your mind wandering? Do you get annoyed by the amount of time it takes your child to express what he is trying to say? Do you tend to multitask (do computer work or check your phone messages) while your child is talking to you?
- Practice listening to your child, trying not to make any judgments or suggestions. Just listen, and if it is helpful, note your observations in your journal.
- Pay attention to what your child says as well as what he leaves out. Sense the kind of mood your child is in. Is he tired, cranky, hungry, or is he ready to engage in conversation? Sometimes timing is everything. With younger children, good times to talk are just after naptime or during snack time because they are less preoccupied with toys and activities. With older children, just before bedtime works well, as this is their time to wind down and reflect on the day.
- When you initiate a conversation with your child, a light touch works best. Make your inquiry casual, rather than probing. It is also helpful to ask specific questions that require more than a yes or no answer, such as, "Tell me about what you and Dena played at day care today."
- When your child talks to you, look at her and make eye contact. A working mother of four said, "By looking at my children directly while they are talking to me, it forces me to take the time to focus on each of them. This way I get to know when something is wrong, or if I am being too intrusive. If I am, I just back off." If a child needs some emotional space, it's best to actively listen while you're doing something simple such as cutting vegetables or folding clothes. It is your job to figure out how to make your child feel comfortable so he can talk and you can listen. Some of us are not as naturally intuitive as others, but with practice, this skill can become better honed for all of us.
- Give your child verbal or physical feedback to let her know that you hear her. A head nod, an "uh-huh", a smile, or a look of concern let her know that you are with her. Try to be aware of your body language. If your body is leaning or twisting away, for example, catching glimpses of a television program, it gives the impression that you do not want to listen.
- Finally, as Atticus Finch said in *To Kill a Mockingbird,* "You never really understand a person until you consider things from his point of view . . . until you climb into his skin and walk around in it." Try to step into your child's skin, even for a moment. Try to appreciate the world from his perspective, his concerns, his hopes and dreams. Listening is the best tool that we have.

Active listening is an art and a skill, and it takes practice. No one ever masters it perfectly. When we are tired, irritable, or overwhelmed, it is, of course, an especially arduous task. Yet, by practicing the art of listening, it can become a regular and helpful part of your interaction with your child. Good listening facilitates good risk-taking. Figure 3.5 offers a checklist to begin your practice of active listening. We recommend that parents simply keep track of their current state of listening for a week or so before proceeding to the next items on the checklist.

In summary, how does active listening impact on your child's ability to take good risks? The answer is that listening well is a building block in the growth of a thoughtful and self-assured child. A child who is *heard* is prepared to put himself in a vulnerable or risky position while attempting to accomplish a difficult challenge much like the edgeworker described in Chapter 1. A risk is approachable if a child knows that his bravery is supported whether he succeeds or fails.

Chapter 4

THE PARENT-CHILD CONNECTION AND THE THREADS OF RISK

We don't accomplish anything in this world alone . . . and whatever happens is the result of the whole tapestry of one's life and all the weavings of individual threads from one to another that creates something.

—*Sandra Day O'Connor*

The development of a child's risk-taking skills is influenced by his temperament, the parent's temperament, and the ongoing parent-child relationship. The parent's history and lifelong experience with risk, and

86

the attitudes and philosophy of the child's school, religious, and community experiences all affect the way a child's risk-taking style develops. These influences work interactively and are defining stitches that are interwoven into a child's psyche.

With recent neurobiological advances in the understanding of brain functioning and behavior, the task of the parent has become simultaneously clearer and more complicated than in previous generations. It is important that we understand that there is not one kind of relationship nor one particular temperamental quality that predicts good risk-taking development. We must understand as much as we can about our children's development, and we need to know how and when we can effect change.

TEMPERAMENT AND RISK-TAKING

Some children are born with a temperament that expresses itself in spontaneous, bold, perhaps impulsive ways, while some come into the world with more tentativeness, cautiousness, and tendency to mull. Today we know that innate temperamental style is among the essential building blocks of personality. Psychiatrists Chess and Thomas (1986, 1996) identified three basic temperamental types of children: easy, difficult, and slow-to-warm-up. They found that each of these temperamental types are composed of nine separate traits including factors such as how adaptable a child is in new situations, how persistent she is, or how distractible he is. They also suggested that children vary, more or less, along a continuum of these nine traits, and with careful observation children can be categorized into one of the three basic temperamental types.

There is also a strong biological basis to temperament. Child psychologist Jerome Kagan and his colleagues (Kagan, 1984, 2006; Kagan & Snidman, 2004) have learned that babies differ in their reactivity to stimuli in the environment, and later, as a result of inborn reactivity styles, they differ along a continuum of inhibition (shy or subdued) to uninhibition (outgoing and social).

They have also found that inborn differences in the amygdala, a structure deep within the brain, as well as individual differences in the hypothalamus, the main structure linking the brain to the hormonal-endocrine system, contribute to these temperamental differences. Since these are two of the parts of the brain that are responsible for the regulation of emotions, it makes sense that individual differences in these brain regions contribute to temperamental differences. Not surprisingly, Chess and Thomas (1996) have reported more recently that their slow-to-warm-up child is similar to Kagan's inhibited child.

This research is important for parents to know because it helps us to better appreciate that our children are born with different temperamental styles and that temperament influences the way our relationship with our child develops. For example, a parent knows that the child who begins to sleep easily and regularly through the night as a young infant is far easier to manage than the colicky infant who keeps you awake all night long. Parenting experts including Stanley Turecki (1985) and Stanley Greenspan (Greenspan & Salmon, 1995) elaborate upon the role of temperament in parenting, and help parents understand and work with their children's sometimes trying temperamental tendencies.

Temperamental differences affect the ongoing connection between parent and child, which in turn influences a child's risk-taking development. In the tradition of Chess, Thomas, Kagan, and others, and from our own work of observing children and their parents over the last 20 years, we have identified seven essential temperamental factors that are essential to the development of risk-taking (see Figure 4.1). Each of these seven factors have a continuum of traits, and they shift and change as the child grows. We know from recent neurobiological research that the brain is far more flexible than was once thought. The human brain is the least developed organ at birth in terms of its complexity (see Gould & Gross, 2002). The brain grows well into young adulthood, well after other organs are fully developed. Scientists are also discovering that the human brain has remarkable flexibility, or plasticity, throughout the life span and brain development is affected by environmental conditions (Doige, 2007). These discoveries are crucial because it lends support to the theory that while each of us is born with a set of temperamental qualities, which are a part of our biological endowment, life's experiences can alter and shift these basic building blocks. Temperament is not as static as it was once thought.

Temperament and the Individual

Parents will attest to the individuality of their children, that they are born with certain traits and tendencies. Parents say, "She was born

---

**FIGURE 4.1. Continuum of Temperamental Factors Essential
to the Development of Risk-Taking**

- Shy, reserved → Gregarious, outgoing
- Cautious → Spontaneous
- Calm and even-keeled→ Emotionally reactive and volatile
- Self-contained and self-sufficient → Socially concerned and involved
- Easy to focus→ Distractible
- Low energy → High energy
- Easily adapts to new situations → Inflexible and rigid

---

stubborn" or "He was outgoing even as an infant," but parents know that these traits can be more or less modified by life's experiences. For example, the child who at age 3 was so shy that he wouldn't talk to anyone but his family, may very well become socially outgoing by high school. Conversely, the spontaneous, outgoing young child can become changed by difficult or stressful life circumstances and may assume a more self-protective stance of reserve and tentativeness when in social situations. Parents also know that traits can change in different circumstances. For example, the child who is spontaneous on the playground may be cautious in the classroom, while the proverbial bookworm may easily contribute to class discussion but be silent and removed in social groups.

Temperamental traits, like most qualities, vary along a continuum of mild to severe (as with an illness), low to high (as in volume or numerically), a little to a lot (as in amount of food heaped on a plate). If a trait falls toward the middle of the continuum, it tends to not be noticed or commented upon. In describing how a child listens and attends to his schoolwork, a teacher may say that a particular child is very focused or is usually distractible. Both ends of the spectrum have their strengths and weaknesses depending on how these behaviors are expressed, or channeled, by the child. For example, a highly focused child can spend hours reading and studying schoolwork, but may have difficulty attending to anything else happening around him. The fire alarm can go off, or the class may end, but the student is still engrossed in his reading, without an awareness that it's time to transition. That's a child on one extreme of the continuum. Another child can be highly distractible, finding it difficult to stay with the teacher's lesson for more than a few minutes. That child may also be able to multitask later on in his life, to observe stock prices, call out bids, and process a multitude of other stimuli on the floor of the New York Stock Exchange. The first child may, more easily than the second, become an accomplished student in school, because of his intense focus, and may end up in a career (e.g., laboratory scientist) that requires that kind of focus. The extremely focused child may need help transitioning from one activity to the next and may always have some trouble adapting to tasks that require different types of attention. The distractible child may have a tougher time as a student and may require help to maintain his attention on schoolwork. He will need to learn how to manage his environment so that he is not over- or understimulated (e.g., see LD OnLine, 1998).

Again, we want to emphasize that not only do these traits fall on a continuum, but they may also be true of a child in some, but not all, situations. A usually shy and self-contained child might be more outgoing and spontaneous on the ball field where his love of the sport—and perhaps his innate talent—lets him "forget himself." A child who is usually distractible in school and at home may be highly focused on the balance beam in gymnastics practice.

CHARLES AND TIFFANY'S STORY

As Tiffany developed, she became increasingly interested in drawing and painting. In fourth grade her teacher—an artist himself—talked to Tiffany and her parents about enrolling Tiffany in some art lessons at the Art Students League in New York City, where they lived. The teacher felt that the level of teaching and commitment of the students would provide an excellent opportunity for Tiffany to develop her talent, and also be among other children who were artistic. He reasoned that this might help Tiffany find some kindred souls, as socializing at school remained difficult for her.

Tiffany was not in favor of this idea because her shy and self-contained style made her reticent to take risks that involve trying something new; putting herself in a new environment was something that she dreaded. In fact, when she and her Dad, Charles, talked about the pros and cons of her attending a weekend art class, Tiffany ran out of the room in tears, pleading, "Stop pushing me, Dad! I'm *not* like you—I don't like trying new things! I hate going places where I don't know anyone!"

Charles, who already had a lot of experience in talking about these issues with Tiffany, wisely let the conversation go for a few days, and then asked her again if she would be willing just to give it a try. He suggested that she sign up for just one class on Saturdays to start. This would give her a chance to step out and take a little risk, but hopefully it would not be overwhelming for her. Very reluctantly she agreed.

When that first Saturday of the still life drawing class came around, Tiffany was so anxious she almost couldn't leave the house. Charles patiently listened to her feelings and tried his best to calm her down. Charles knew that this was a substantial risk for Tiffany.

Unfortunately, despite the fact that it was a good risk, things didn't go so well for Tiffany that morning. She cried all the way to the Art Students League and stayed for the class only after Charles lost his temper with her. After the first class Tiffany told her father that she was too nervous to continue going to the art school. She said that her hands were shaking the whole time and she couldn't talk to anyone. Charles was disappointed but careful not to show this to Tiffany. He wanted to respect Tiffany's feelings, and he knew that if he lost his temper again it wouldn't help either of them.

Reluctantly, Charles waited several months, but he continued to think about ways to encourage Tiffany to go to art class. He suggested that they ask her cousin, who was about the same age and also interested in art, to sign up for the class and go along with Tiffany. Perhaps that might help her feel more comfortable. This extra support helped Tiffany feel less anxious, and she was able to continue in the art class, although with some starts and stops. Eventually, after a year or so, she was able to take classes without someone accompanying her.

This story about Tiffany's struggles is but one example how temperament affects risk-taking. Another child would not be fazed by the prospect of signing up for an after-school class without a friend, but would be almost paralyzed by the fear of raising his hand in class: This child may feel insecure about his intellectual abilities or be fearful of making a mistake and seeming foolish. Yet another child might be frightened of sleeping anywhere other than her own home, so that overnight stays at friends or relatives would be impossible or painful: This child has difficulty being separated from her parents.

Every child's profile of strengths and weaknesses has its unique configuration, and parents need to be savvy about their child's style to best guide him in his development. Development takes time, and it needs to unfold partially on its own terms, and partially via parental guidance and support. Charles felt disappointed that Tiffany gave up on the art classes after only one session, and that his own fiery temperament interfered with his ability to be patient with her.

In this vignette, we see that the differences of temperament between the father and daughter clashed at one point, but Charles, who had done a lot of self-reflective work, backed off after losing his temper. He eventually waited patiently and intervened wisely to help Tiffany take the leap toward accomplishment and mastery that was consistent with her temperamental style.

What Do Parents Bring to the Mix?

Our temperamental styles—whether we are reserved or gregarious, emotionally volatile or even-keeled, cautious or spontaneous, distractible or focused, adaptable or rigid, or highly energetic or relaxed—influence our child's risk-taking development. Our life experiences, hurdles, trauma, parenting, and schooling have impacted upon who we've become and the parent we are.

From the very beginning we enter into a relationship with our child that is unique and reciprocal. We know that we are different with our 3-year-old daughter than we are with our 6-year-old son. It's more than just developmental stage and gender; it's the complex process of how each has connected with the other from our child's infancy.

What dictates these important differences? Is it the parent's own temperament and personality? Is it a function of the parent's own childhood experiences, or is it due to current factors in the parent's life, such as the current level of stress? What about issues such as financial problems, or occupational and marital stressors? Do these issues also affect a parent's capacity to tolerate and respond effectively through the emotional stresses involved in parenting? The answer is that it is all of these factors that can be responsible, in varying ways and amounts, for the way a given parent-child relationship unfolds.

THE PARENT-CHILD FIT AND RISK

The "fit," or match, between parent and child also affects the development of risk-taking. There is a body of literature that also comes from Chess and Thomas's (1996) seminal longitudinal study. In addition to analyzing children's temperamental traits statistically to yield three temperamental types, they also developed a brilliant, and useful, concept of "fit" between child and parent. Essentially, *fit* is the way in which the parent's temperament interacts with the child's temperament. "Goodness of fit" is determined by the healthy functioning of the child; in other words, a child who is on track in his development is functioning well in social, school, and intellectual tasks. Fit can be modified over time by understanding the child's temperamental style, one's own temperamental style, and by working to accommodate the child to improve the match.

Parents and children continually affect one another in profound ways. For example, your first child, now 6, may have been a baby with whom you could relate easily—he may have been placid, easy to soothe, and able to sleep through the night. His younger sister, now 3 years old, was colicky and difficult to soothe. These differing traits lead to different reactions on your part and on the part of your child; over time, these reactions become part of the template of your connection with your child.

If, for example, you are particularly sensitive to the unrelenting and pain-filled cries of your colicky child, you may unwittingly shy away from holding her closely. You may feel impatient and have a hard time soothing her piercing cries. In contrast, if your baby's crying is not so upsetting that you feel undone by it because of your temperament, you may be better equipped to respond to your infant with more calm, empathy, and soothing.

Using this example, we can better understand the concept of goodness of fit. First, if you identify with the parent who finds it hard to connect with her baby because of her constant, piercing cries, you must become aware that this is how you are feeling. Second, you must be patient with yourself and not judge yourself harshly. If you do find yourself unable to soothe your baby as well as you'd like, then applying the practices of self-reflection and listening is the first step toward making a change.

As discussed in Chapter 3, these skills can help you understand how your child is affecting you and also help you think through your emotional discomfort so that you can move toward a better fit with your child. Perhaps, you come to realize that your shrieking baby reminds you of your own feelings of helpless that you had as a child and how you never felt soothed enough. Understanding the roots of your feelings, though, can only go so far. Even when you understand why your baby gets to you, you may still feel that you don't know how to make a change. We have found that after doing the work of self-reflection, parents are usually ready to make practical changes.

To return to our example, perhaps you can get some support for the hours that the baby cries. Asking your spouse, friend, or family member to help out during these times can significantly ease the stress. Or, if you know that you are particularly agitated when you get little sleep, you can schedule naps in the afternoon while your baby sleeps. You may also realize that your baby's cries unleash so much discomfort that you need to talk to a confidante or a professional to uncover and understand the emotional reaction. Many women join mothers' groups where they bring their babies and talk among themselves. This is a good way to get emotional support and make valuable connections with other mothers. Women listen to each other's trials and wisdom, and have a sounding board for their own frustrations and worries. Just connecting with others and learning that there is a wide range of normal reactions to these everyday situations can be so helpful.

What is crucial here is the process that the parent begins, in which she is moving toward deeper self-awareness and a better understanding of who her child is—with all his imperfections. Over time, this process of awareness on the part of the parent allows the parent to better accommodate her child's style and move toward a better parent-child fit.

JUDY AND HANNAH'S STORY

In applying the concept of fit between parent and child to the development of risk-taking, we need to look simultaneously at parent and child to see how the threads of traits and experiences configure and interact. Judy and Hannah provide a good illustration. Judy's childhood experiences combined with her inborn temperamental style created a mom who was thoughtful, nonimpulsive, nurturing, and sometimes restrained and passive. She would not be described as a robust risk-taker, although she was able to understand that positive risk-taking is healthy and important. Remember, she had even conquered her fears about skiing to become a decent skier. In her work she was able to promote smart risks for her students and their parents.

When it came to her own child, Hannah, she sometimes still had difficulty seeing her tendency to be overprotective and overly cautious. Despite her progress toward being an authoritative parent she still at times felt incompetent and ineffective in the face of Hannah's impulsive risk-taking style, a style that emerged largely from Hannah's temperamental style of high energy, emotional volatility, and spontaneity. She admired Hannah's moxie, but felt challenged in helping her daughter channel her behavior into smart risk-taking.

This is a fit that might be considered a mismatch because of the mother and daughter's different temperaments, coupled with the mother's history of fear and caution in her own rearing. However, with self-reflection Judy was able to see how her tendency toward overprotectiveness was affecting her daughter. This made it easier to see her daughter's temperamental traits in a clearer light and work toward better understanding her behavior. Over time, as Judy became more mindful of her own tentative style, she learned to set clearer and more authoritative limits on Hannah's behavior. Sometimes she even joined Hannah as she went down the slide and jumped on the trampoline. Judy and Hannah began to communicate more comfortably about when to "go for it" and when to pull back. As a result, the fit between mother and child improved, and Judy guided Hannah's development as a smart risk-taker more effectively.

Judy's development as a more authoritative—and constructively limit-setting—parent evolved over time. To be sure, it was not easy for her, and there were baby steps forward along with many missteps. This is often the norm because change is difficult to accomplish and habits are resistant to change. It is a challenging task to see oneself clearly. However, Judy was resolute in her desire to be a more effective parent to Hannah and to help her take thoughtful steps ahead.

She found that Hannah clearly responded to the subtle and not-so-subtle attempts to understand her, and she responded to firm, safe boundaries. As Hannah felt more understood, her need to be provocative diminished, and she became somewhat calmer. While she became more receptive to her mother's input, Hannah also remained Hannah. She maintained her high energy, and she would rather *do* than sit and think. At times, Judy still became frustrated and frightened by Hannah's risk-taking style, and she learned that no matter what she did, Hannah found it hard to think before she leapt. Yet over time Hannah would learn to make smarter and more conservative steps forward.

HOW THIS ALL BEGINS:
UNDERSTANDING ATTACHMENT AND RISK

Reciprocity, the crucial give-and-take of all relationships, is absolutely vital for the developing child and his parent. There is an intricate dance that takes place from birth. Here the saying "it takes two to tango" is absolutely true, and on a deep level. This dance is another fundamental component of the development of risk, and has been studied by infant-caregiver researchers (see Beebe & Lachmann, 1988; Beebe & Sloate, 1982; Bowlby, 1988; Stern, 1985).

These psychological researchers have captured on videotape the ways in which the mother, or primary caregiver, from the moment of the child's birth, gazes at her baby, and the baby gazes back at her. It used to be thought that there was a one-way interaction between the pair, that it was the mother who affected the baby by unilaterally teaching and modeling behavior. The mother was thought of as the dominant creative force in the duo. Today, we know that parent and child shape each other: The baby affects the caregiver, and the caregiver affects the baby (see Fonagy, Gergely, Jurist, & Target, 2002).

This is the dance of connection, emotional regulation, and attachment. These early interactions are a template—a foundation or a cognitive-emotional map—for later relationships. They set the stage for the reciprocity in relationship that happens throughout life. During the many moments when the mother makes eye contact and coos at her infant, baby looks back at her, matching her visual contact. The mother then encourages, raising her voice to a higher pitch to begin a playful exchange. The baby continues to hold his mother's gaze, but then looks away after a few moments. Trying to engage more, she tries a new voice pitch and when he is reengaged, talks to him in this new pitch.

She experiments with different pitches, intensities, rhythms of vocal expression, and exaggerated facial expressions to engage her child and further the pleasure of the interaction with her baby. He coos more when the combination of her voice, facial expression, and touch stimulates him just so, and looks away when the interaction no longer interests him or becomes overstimulating, intrusive, or too repetitive. If the mother persists in a manner that is unwanted or is felt to be intrusive or unpleasant, the infant withdraws. Ideally, mother assesses her baby's reaction and responds accordingly while the baby takes it all in. Mother learns from infant, and the infant learns from mother.

With a less sensitive or less intuitive parent, one can imagine how the parent-infant interaction might occur. Maybe the mother is passive and waits for the baby to gaze at her, and then she'll return her gaze. Maybe she will try interactive behaviors that are too loud or abrasive, and the infant will cry, signaling that he is uncomfortable, overstimulated, or frightened. What if the parent doesn't read the cues correctly and tries repeatedly to make the baby smile by the same singing or rocking methods used before? This type of interplay creates a different template for the parent-child attachment, one of less attunement. *Attunement* is the process wherein caregivers constantly adjust their stimulation of an infant—for example, in baby talk and play—in response to signs from the infant (DeHart, Sroute, & Cooper, 2004), In a parent-child pair in which there is less attunement, the child learns over time that his reactions and behaviors don't lead to gratification or pleasurable connection.

Mother and infant continually play and learn from each other. This is what is meant when scientists say that they are "shaping" each other's behavior. A parent and a toddler, preschooler, elementary-school-age child, preadolescent and adolescent do much the same, but the dance is based on prior learning from each sequential developmental stage and is impacted by experience from all facets of life (home, school, friendships, and so on). It occurs from what is said and not said between parent and child. This is the cycle of attachment—the process of mutually or reciprocally influencing, connecting, and imprinting upon each other.

This happens consciously and unconsciously, through words and through gesture. It is important for parents to realize that this process can never be perfect, nor should it be. As discussed earlier, the connection just has to be "good enough" (Winnicott, 1953). If it were even possible to always meet our child's needs and desires, this would not be optimal. This child could never learn frustration tolerance, nor could he manage on his own.

ATTACHMENT AND RISK BEYOND INFANCY

Researchers have looked at the attachment between mother (or caregiver) and child in many different ways (see Ainsworth, 1969; Beebe & Lachmann, 1988; Bowlby, 1969; Fonagy et al., 2002; Fonagy & Target,

2005; Sroufe, 1985). Our understanding of emotional attachment between parents and their infants has shifted drastically over the last 40
years (Karen, 1998).

In the earlier part of the twentieth century it was believed that
our children were not affected long-term by experiences that occur in
infancy. Whatever was "forgotten" or not accessible to memory and
couldn't be verbally recounted supposedly had no impact or formative
power on the child's behavior or personality. Behaviorists like John
Watson (1914) advised parents to treat their children strictly and un-
emotionally, lest they "spoil" them. *Spoiling* a child referred to allowing them to express (or "indulge in") feelings and show dependency
on their caregivers.

During the 1960's this parenting outlook began to change in our
society. Earlier on, psychiatrist John Bowlby had addressed the importance of tenderness and the necessity of attachment between parent
and child. In a powerfully seminal work, he wrote about children who
were separated from their parents during lengthy hospital stays. He
studied the harmful emotional and physical effects of such separations
and went on to create a large body of work on parent-child attachment
that had a huge impact on the field of mental health, parenting, developmental psychology, and psychotherapy.

Mary Ainsworth next took up the study of attachment (e.g., 1969;
Ainsworth, Belar, Water, & Walls, 1978), creating a laboratory research
design that allowed for empirical study. In what she called the "Strange
Situation," she put mothers and infants in a series of laboratory situations where their behavior, reactions, and relationship styles could be
looked at and analyzed statistically according to research guidelines.
Initially, Ainsworth and colleagues had gone into the parents' homes
and watched how the mothers held and responded to their young babies when they cried and fussed. They observed the attachment patterns of mothers and their babies in several visits over the first year of
the babies' lives and made assessments as to whether the babies were
securely or insecurely attached to their parent, based on the infant's
response to the style of parenting.

Then Ainsworth and her colleagues created a laboratory study that
they hoped would be able to distinguish parents' and children's types
of attachment patterns. They observed mother, child, and an unfamiliar adult in various combinations by way of a one-way mirror. The
research paradigm involved a mother and baby together in an unfa-

miliar room that has toys around to engage the child in exploration and play. They observed how the mother and infant interact together and in relation to the toys. Does the child toddle away to play with the toys, and does he look back at mom to make sure she's there, or does he stay next to her? Does the parent engage in play with her child and the toys, or is the child reluctant to leave the mother's lap? Next the mother leaves the room and the child is observed in how he reacts to this separation. Does he cry or is he unperturbed? Then the mother returns to the room. How does the infant react? With pleasure and an approach initiating contact? Or does the child exhibit anger, crying, or disinterest? Next a stranger comes in while the mother is still in the room. How does the baby respond to the stranger—with fear and crying or with interest and interaction with the stranger? The next situation involves the mother leaving again, while the stranger is still there. Is the infant frightened? What does he do? When the mother returns a second time, how does the infant react? With anger and crying, or pleasurable relief? Is the child consolable, or does he continue to be upset and reject the parent's comfort?

Ainsworth and colleagues found that by analyzing the data of these patterns of behaviors in response to maternal separation, children fell into distinctive categories of attachment. Children were seen as either "securely attached" or "insecurely attached," with two subsets labeled "ambivalent" and "avoidant." She found that the mothers of the "securely attached" group of children were significantly more responsive to them—quicker to pick them up when they are distressed, to hold them with warmth and pleasure, and to be emotionally expressive. They were rated as being more sensitive, accepting, and emotionally available to their children. The mothers of the "insecurely attached" group rated lower on the measures of emotional responsivity. The mothers of the "ambivalent" group of children showed more unpredictability in behavior toward their infants, while the mothers of the "avoidant" group were significantly more rejecting.

Ainsworth's work led other researchers to look at attachment patterns as the child grows older. Alan Sroufe and his colleagues conducted what is known as the "Minnesota Studies" to determine if these descriptions of early attachment patterns hold up over time (Sroufe, Egeland, Carlson, & Collins, 2005). They devised play activities that were appropriate for 18-month-old children and observed them in play with their mothers in the room. They found that the "securely attached" children were better able to moderate their impulses, showed positive feelings like enthusiasm and persistence, and showed less frustration. The "securely attached" children engaged in more symbolic play (imaginary play with dolls and pretending), which is regarded as a sign of healthy emotional and cognitive development. Correspondingly, the mothers of the "securely attached" children were observed to be more supportive and less intrusive in the play.

Mothers of the "insecurely attached" children became intrusive at times, giving direction or actually doing the task for the child. They were less willing to tolerate their child's frustrations. Some of the mothers, on the other hand, stayed separate from the play, offering no words of encouragement or support.

Other studies on somewhat older children were also done, showing that at age 3½, the "securely attached" group were better related socially and more empathic to peers (Sroufe et al., 2005). Other studies indicate that these findings hold true throughout childhood and beyond (Grossman, Grossman, & Waters, 2005).

These studies support the importance of a parenting philosophy that lays the foundations for a child to feel securely attached. These studies do not, however, take into consideration temperamental differences among children. Some children are born with temperaments that include sensitivity to frustration, high levels of reactivity, variable moods, and slowness in adapting to new situations. These temperamental traits would cause such children to have a difficult time in the stranger situation despite the parent's style of parenting. Jerome Kagan (Kagan & Snidman, 2004) and his colleagues at Harvard studied the role of biological factors and assert that children are born with certain traits that heavily determine their personality. He contended that environmental factors such as parenting style have much less impact on the child than the attachment researchers believe.

How can parents use these findings to better understand their children's development and to encourage good risk-taking? Nowadays we are aware of an intricate balance of many factors that affect a child's growth and development. We know that temperament plays an important part in development, but so does the child's environment, which includes parenting style, attachment, home environment (siblings, financial stresses), physical health, personal trauma, and school and community influences. The research on attachment and temperament are equally important in understanding how children grow and develop. Today, we know that understanding the threads of temperament and attachment are helpful for us to understand our child's development and, more specifically, to guide his risk-taking development.

THE NEUROBIOLOGY OF RISK

In recent years we have learned a lot about the neurobiology of many aspects of human emotional life (LeDoux, 1996; Solms, 1997, 2000). This research is germane for parents who want to understanding the underpinnings of attachment and risk. Neurobiologists and neuropsychologists use the latest medical and imaging technology (including MRI, PET scan, and electrophysical studies) to provide evidence that there are specific regions of the brain that are central to the attachment process. For example, Alan Schore and his colleagues (Bradshaw & Schore, 2007; Schore, 2002a, 2002b, 2005; Schore & Schore, 2008), who have looked extensively at human and animal populations, have found that the structures within the right side of the brain (known as the right hemisphere) are key in the establishment of the connection between caregiver and baby. The right side of the brain is the hemisphere that is largely responsible for the expression and regulation of emotion, creativity, and nonverbal problem solving.

It is also important to understand that the structures situated at the surface of the brain (cortical based) are responsible for higher order functioning including problem solving, while structures situated deeper within the brain (subcortical) are responsible for more primitive functioning including maintaining vital body physiology and emotion. According to Schore (2002b), the highest order emotional processing takes place in the right cortex, in particular, in the right frontal lobe. He writes, "[It is] referred to as the thinking part of the emotional brain. . . . This senior executive of the social-emotional brain comes to act in the capacity of an executive control function for the entire right brain, the locus of the emotional self" (p. 14). Within the subcortical structures lies the limbic system, in which emotion is processed and regulated. One important part of the limbic system that regulates vital functions, stress, and emotion is called the *amygdala.* The amygdala has strong connections with the autonomic and central nervous system.

From this research we learn not only that there are specific regions of the brain that are active during emotional processing but also that there are structural brain differences based on a person's ability to connect with others, and to manage (self-regulate) his feelings. Not surprisingly, A. N. Schore and J. R. Schore (2008) found that "attachment experiences shape the early organization of the right brain, the neurobiological core of the human unconscious" (p. 10). This means that the baby's earliest relationship with her caregiver impacts upon the child's brain development. Yet it has also been found that even if early organization of the right brain is not optimal (e.g., due to trauma or illness) the psychotherapeutic relationship and other human relationships are effective later on in actually altering the neural patterns in these parts of the brain for the better (see Fonagy & Target, 2002; Linden, 2006; Schore, 2001). To reiterate, these findings are consistent with what we now know about the brain's plasticity, or flexibility, over time.

Taken together with earlier research on temperament and attachment, Schore's studies have important implications for the development of risk-taking because we now have evidence that strongly suggests that the very organization and functioning of parts of our brains can change as a result of our earliest and ongoing human relationships and experiences in the world.

This implies that the child who is naturally cautious can become a good risk-taker. And conversely, the child who is prone to taking risks can become more inhibited over time. What we have learned from neurobiological research is that the social interactions, emotions, thoughts, and behaviors of humans from infancy onward become encoded in the brain by virtue of their neurochemical and structural counterparts. Healthy attachment between a parent and child has a profound impact on the child's neural circuitry and biological functioning and furthers maturation in positive, progressive ways. Trauma, particularly ongoing traumas such as neglect, abuse, or serious emotional loss, inhibit maturation and create insecure and disorganized attachment or connections with others, and as well has neurobiological consequences.

Children are born with a given temperamental-biological endowment. The environment (including important early relationships) affects the developing brain and interacts with temperament to create a mind-body entity that is a road map for personality. The child-parent relationship is crucial in creating a well-functioning road map for life. Most positive in this confirming new evidence is that new behaviors, thoughts, and interactions—if they persist and become integrated—can actually modify the brain's imprinted map and thus bring about positive changes in social, emotional, and intellectual functioning.

This means that a poor fit between parent and child can be worked on and improved. This also means that a child with behavioral and emotional difficulties can be helped through thoughtful, active interventions. Sadly, it also means that formative years of neglect and abuse create a template for poor functioning. However, templates are not irreversible. Effective behavioral and emotional interventions can create changed brains and thus changed feelings, thoughts, and behaviors. Of course, there are limits to the optimism of this perspective, as children with severe disabilities of biological origin may need more than environmental or behavioral interventions. One can hypothesize that this is true as well of children with severe and lengthy traumatic experiences. Sometimes medication and other treatments are needed (e.g., for severe attentional or mood disorders). More severe disabilities (such as those on the autistic spectrum, and with severe or profound mental retardation) can be helped by appropriate environmental effort; however, the goals tend to be more modest.

HOW DOES THIS ALL COME TOGETHER?

How do our studies of attachment, temperament, parent-child fit, parental history, and parental self-reflection come together to inform us about good risk-taking? All of these factors are intricately woven into the creation of a child's base of security about himself and his abilities, his relationships with others, and the world around him. Children who grow from a secure parent-child connection are more prepared to believe in themselves and to thoughtfully enact positive risks. Taking good risks initiates a positive cycle for children. Good risk-taking feels good, and the child will want to repeat this feeling. For example, the shy child who speaks up in class for the first time feels the pride, satisfaction, and generally positive emotions associated with this leap. Good risk-takers become better able to tolerate the uneasy feelings of leaving their place of comfort and risking possible failure. This entails an internalization of the secure attachment with the parent; the child knows that he can manage and regulate his feelings, and he finds comfort and support through what he has learned in his early interactions with his parent. This internalization allows the child to know that he is resilient; he can persevere through a failure and eventually try again, or try something new.

What We Can Do

We can help our children become good risk-takers, no matter what our initial connection is like. As parents, we must recognize that what we say and do—as well as what we do not do and do not say—all impact our children's concept of themselves and the world around them. Through the important process of self-reflection, we become aware of the messages we are teaching our children. The ways in which parents seize the moment, move forward in their life, and model decisions about what risks are worth or not worth taking, are communicated to their children. There are corresponding brain changes that take place based on what the children learn, what they feel, and how they consequentially behave. The brain is the seat of all emotions and behaviors. This is an important concept for parents to understand. There are different kinds of brains. Children come into this world with a certain biological endowment. It is our responsibility as parents to work with our children and create a "good-enough" fit, to guide them to become emotionally and socially intelligent (Goleman, 1995, 2006), and to teach and model smart risk-taking skills. These are the skills that enable children to soar through life. We also know that while long-term adverse conditions can hamper the child's risk-taking potential, recent research has repeatedly found that the brain is far more adaptable than was thought in previous centuries (Doidge, 2007).

It is through the process of mutual attachment between parent and child that the child learns many of life's fundamental lessons: how to love and be loved, how to trust and be trusted, how to appreciate another human being, how to be appreciated, and how to appreciate himself.

It is helpful to reflect upon the present state of your relationship with your child to nurture this connection. Figure 4.2 describes how to do this.

What Do I Do If My Child and I Are Mismatched?

Since we have made the case that a "good-enough" fit and rapport between parent and child set the stage for a positive risk-taking style, how can the parent, who is presently dissatisfied with the state of his connection to his child, make the necessary changes? We have found that this work follows naturally from the process of self-reflection and listening. Similar to, and continuing the processes begun in Chapter 2, the practice of observing and recording one's actions and reactions is an excellent beginning to making the desired changes. And it is never too late to begin to make a change.

LOUIS AND CHRIS'S STORY

Remember that Louis had practiced self-reflection and listening while his son Chris was in preschool and kindergarten. This work helped him be a little more patient and understanding with Chris, although Chris's "lack of fire" still bothered him. As Chris grew older it became easier for both of them to let Chris hang out with his mother, Liz, so he and his son could avoid the negative feelings that they sometimes had when they were together.

Eventually, Chris began to resent the fact that his father didn't spend much time with him. Chris didn't say anything about this to his parents, because Chris didn't quite realize it himself. The problem became apparent as Chris's behavior erupted at home. Chris would constantly torment his younger brother, and he would not listen to his parents' demands at home. For example, when Louis shouted from the other room, "Stop playing, Chris, and clean up for dinner," Chris would ignore him until Louis lost his temper. Chris would also try to get attention from his father by acting out. One time he "accidentally" dropped—and broke—an expensive watch of Louis's. Then he said sarcastically, "Too bad that broke, Dad; you must care more about that watch than you do about me."

Louis and Liz were at their wits' end. When Louis finally reflected upon the quality of his current relationship with Chris, he did not feel proud of the job he was doing as a parent. Louis realized that he found Chris to be annoying and an embarrassing nuisance. He realized that while he had "bent over backwards" to accommodate his son's "style" in preschool and kindergarten, he just couldn't maintain this attitude. Louis realized that he felt that Chris was, in his own words, "a big disappointment."

Louis wrote in his journal, "How could I have a kid so different from me? And that kid doesn't know how good he has it! He has *never* put his all into anything—and when he broke that watch, it was a good thing Liz was there or I would have really lost it with him."

It became obvious to Louis that by unknowingly communicating these feelings to Chris, he was setting up a relationship in which Chris would act out and take bad risks, such as "accidentally" breaking the

---

FIGURE 4.2. Reflection About Parent-Child Connection

- How much time do you spend alone (one-on-one) with your child per day/per week?
- How do you spend this time together? How much time is spent in obligatory activities such as dong homework together? How much time is spent together in mutually enjoyable and playful activities? How many meals per week do you have together?
- What is the quality of this time? How much time is spent in conflict with each other—yelling and nagging? How much time is silly or playful or fun? How much time is educational, instructive, and serious?
- Do you look forward to spending time with your child, do you dread it, or do you feel something in between?
- How do you feel about the balance between time spent at work and time spent with your child? Does your child feel the same way you do?
- Do you generally feel proud of your child? Do you feel that she is likable and fun to be with? Or are you generally disappointed and ashamed of her?
- Which of of your child's traits are most admirable? Which traits do you most frequently criticize? Why?
- Do you have interests similar to your child's?

---

watch. This time around, Louis decided to talk to Chris to find some activity that they could enjoy doing together. They knew that they had to stay away from doing sports or any endeavor in which Louis's competitive spirit would be engaged. Finally, they decided to build small model cars together. At first, Chris wasn't so sure that he wanted to risk the interaction with his Dad again. Every time he tried, it had backfired. His Dad would end up criticizing his efforts, and that ruined the fun. At first, Chris would angrily—and intentionally—ruin each model they worked on together. He would "accidentally" spill the paint they needed or would get glue on the kitchen table. Louis tried very hard not to criticize Chris, but stated calmly and quietly that he should try to be more careful next time. Louis also made Chris responsible for the cleanup of his messes.

Over time, though, model building became an activity that they both enjoyed, and Chris's behavior improved. Louis admired Chris's ability to manipulate and paint the small parts of the cars, and Chris felt the positive effects of his Dad's admiration. While the benefits of this activity didn't generalize to other areas until much later, it was at least a good start for both of them.

The Threads of Risk

This story about Chris and Louis illustrates that it is the subtle combination of a lot of factors, including temperament and the goodness of fit between parent and child, that contributes to the development of a secure parent-child connection from which the child can learn to take good risks. This story shows how this develops over time, and why Chris, at age 8, was avoiding taking positive risks, especially in his father's presence. He wanted to please his father, but the differences between them made it too risky for him to show his vulnerabilities and to open himself to his father's seemingly inevitable criticism. Through a mutually enjoyable activity, over time and with patience, Chris began to take the risks that began to convince his Dad of his competence in model building. Chris and Louis will probably never share many of the same interests; Louis may have to continue to live with the fact that Chris is not "a chip off the old block." Yet, despite their temperamental differences, their differences in neurobiological wiring, and in their upbringing and expectation, Louis was able to play a vital role in helping Chris develop a positive risk-taking style.

In this chapter we have shown that your child's risk-taking style is strongly influenced by temperament and the parent-child temperamental match. In turn, these threads influence the evolving connection between you and your child. There are also a number of other influences that affect the parent-child relationship and risk-taking development. These include learning or other developmental issues, physical illness, or environmental situations such as divorce or a family's financial stresses.

Chapter 5

RISK-TAKING IN SCHOOL

Creativity requires the courage to let go of certainties.

—*Erich Fromm*

In one fourth-grade class there is an activity that takes place every day for the last 20 minutes of school. It's called "Hanging with Dave," and during this time the children can talk about fun subjects with their teacher, David. David is a funny, personable man, who runs a structured and academically rigorous classroom. The children raise their hands and talk about their experiences and ideas, ask David questions, and learn how to speak openly in a public forum. The purpose of this activity is to become comfortable with sharing ideas that are neither right nor wrong, and to speak up where there is minimal possibility of failing.

Why is "Hanging with Dave" an example of risk taking? What possible risk could there be in sharing a story about your baby sister or about your after-school basketball game? As we have pointed out in previous chapters, there are risks inherent in public speaking. The speaker runs the risk of embarrassing himself in any number of ways: not correctly remembering the events, others not finding the story amusing, even the possibility of passing gas while speaking. To stand up and share something personal—even in the comfort of a hangout session created by a trusted and well-respected teacher—is a risk. The children are eager to take on this risk because they trust and like their teacher. Risk-taking becomes safe and fun, and the children feel proud, gratified, and successful when they participate. The overarching goal of this activity is to help children learn to take risks that can be applied to more challenging academic and social situations.

THE FOUNDATION OF LEARNING

This chapter focuses on risk-taking and school (Holt, Stamell, & Field, 1996; Newton, 1996). Parents can take an active role in partnering with teachers to encourage good risk-taking. Learning is a cornerstone of risk for our children. There are the inevitable doubts: "What if I can't do it?" "What if I fail?" "What if I embarrass myself?" Good risk-taking behavior prevails above doubt in a classroom climate of safety (e.g., "My teacher Dave will support me if I slip up"). And learning something new brings joyful feelings of pride, ("Yay, I did it!"), mastery ("I know how to do that now"), and self-esteem ("I'm a can-do person"). When the process goes well, the pride, mastery, and self-esteem become very powerful incentives that propel children to take more risks and to move ahead in their development.

Over the course of a child's school career, each of the universal emotional risks is encountered at one time or another. As we discussed in Chapter 2, there are six universal risks:

- The risk of achievement and mastery
- The risk of separation from the the primary caregiver

- The risk of enduring delayed gratification
- The risk of social and emotional connection with others
- The risk of expressing one's beliefs, convictions, knowledge, and ideas
- The risk of struggling with uncertainty

The risk of feeling incompetent while moving toward achievement is ubiquitous. Children across the developmental spectrum also risk the feeling of aloneness as they function separately, and independently, from their caregivers in school. They must learn to delay gratification as they learn to take turns with their peers, and to delay shouting out in class. The risk of rejection looms large, especially on the playground and in group situations with peers. As a child matures cognitively, the risk of denigration increases as the child expresses increasingly complicated personal beliefs and ideas. And finally, within the school environment the child must learn to sit with feeling uneasy. This ranges from the uncertainty a preschooler experiences as she waits for her father to pick her up from school to the feelings associated with the possibility of rejection that the fifth-grader must manage after trying out for the lead in the school play.

When introducing children to learning—from teaching them how to grasp a fork or hold a pencil to helping them with their first spelling test—it is helpful for parents (and teachers) to focus on the joy of achievement. It's fun to have new experiences, and it feels good to know new things. The main ingredients in early learning are fun, creativity, and play.

However, there are certain "leaps of faith," or risks, that children have to take to get to a next stage in their learning. For example, when a parent leaves her child in her nursery school class for the first time, the child (as well as the parent) is taking a risk. The child doesn't know for sure that things will be fine without mommy, and mommy doesn't know for sure that her child will be happy without her. (She may know it in her mind, but not necessarily in her heart.) This is the risk: Should I go ahead and do something that I don'tknow will work out fine? To learn this important concept the risk must be taken. By taking this risk the child learns that things can be safe and fun, even if mommy is not in the room. And the parent can learn that her child can be safe and happy, even if she is not there to watch her. Through this risk, both parent and child learn that accomplishment and mastery are pleasurable, and the child moves toward growth and independence.

Risk-Taking Starts Early

As discussed, the process of teaching your child to take risks in learning starts early in life, from the time he toddles a short distance from you to begin exploring the world around him. At this stage the parent's reactions are pivotal. For example, as the toddler heads toward the electrical socket, it is time to pick him up (calmly) and move him (gently) to another spot, saying, "Don't touch. That socket is dangerous." Limits need to be set; yet, if your child senses that you are anxious and upset, rather than concerned, he gets an implicit message saying, "Alert! Risk is bad! Don't move away from Mommy!" If he learns, through your worried parental tone, that toddling away, not the socket, is what is dangerous, then this begins to influence the formation of his risk-taking style.

In contrast, if he gets the message that touching a socket is dangerous, not toddling, he gets a different message about safety and risk. This is also true of a lot of everyday experiences such as learning how to cut his own food. Knives can be dangerous, but learning how to cut his own food while being supervised is not. These are the daily interactions that are the blueprints for later risk-taking in learning. The child who learns early on that the world is a dangerous place will have more difficulty taking good risks—no matter what his temperamental nature—than the child who learns that the world is a safe place in which to take risks. This is because he has internalized the messages inherent in doubt and fear.

Risks Are Everywhere

Risks are inherent in every learning challenge, from raising a hand to answer a question in first grade, to deciding to stay home from a get-together with friends to study for a test in high school. It is a risk for the 10-year-old boy to put himself in the position of being called a wimp when he auditions for the school play. It is a risk for a 9-year-old girl to speak up against a strong clique of mean girls. There is also the risk of writing an essay you really care about, putting your time and hard work into it, and admitting to yourself and others that you really care how it turns out. These are the risks of putting yourself on the line and admitting that you have put your all into it. It is reaching into the unknown—without knowing if you are going to succeed or fail.

However, as discussed in previous chapters, failure needs to be recognized as a normal part of life. Children can only learn to take positive risks when they (and their parents) come to know that they can survive the disappointment and the pain of the failure. Missteps hover in every possible situation. A child thinks she knows the answer, but she remembers it inaccurately. Or a budding flutist overtightens her ambusher, and the sounds come out muted when she begins playing her piece. Sometimes a child practices his shooting and dribbling skills day and night, and he still doesn't make the basketball team. Sometimes all the practice or study in the world won't prevent a failed outcome. Failure happens.

Sometimes failure can even lead us in new and serendipitous directions. For example, highly successful people often say that it was their failures, such as being fired from a job, that taught them invaluable information and skills. Our failures often help us develop better judgment and persevere beyond where we ever imagined would be possible.

LOUIS AND CHRIS'S STORY

Chris was finishing third grade when his teacher contacted Louis and Liz again. It seemed that a new problem had arisen. Chris was never much of a "go-getter" (as Louis would say), but he was an adequate student. He learned to read and write easily in the first and second grades and learned his rudimentary arithmetic facts without much effort or problem. Then, one day his teacher called, saying, "Chris is doing poorly in math, and I am not sure if he is going to pass."

Liz and Louis were shocked—and worried. "What happened?" they wondered. They knew that he seemed quieter than usual, but they thought that this was just another passing phase.

When Liz and Louis spoke to the teacher, she helped them to understand that the recent class work in mathematics had become significantly more complicated. They were working on concepts that required the students to manipulate difficult spatial relationships. They were focusing, for example, on learning volume and mass and geometric concepts. "He just seems to tune out," said the teacher. "He can't seem to focus, and he won't ask me for help." She continued by saying, " I consulted with the school psychologist who recommended that you consider having a psychoeducational assessment so we all have a better understanding of what is going on."

The teacher explained that psychoeducational assessments are administered by a licensed psychologist and examine a person's intellectual, academic, and emotional functioning to help teachers and parents understand the child's learning strengths and weaknesses. This is sometimes very important in figuring out how best to help a child who is having difficulties in school.

Louis and Liz agreed and got the names of a few private psychologists and a nonprofit service agency that did learning evaluations for children, but they felt devastated. "More problems! Testing is expensive!" shouted Louis. When they got home, the situation went from bad to worse. Louis shouted at Chris for not trying hard enough and for not paying attention in class. Liz then shouted at Louis for being too hard on Chris.

The next few weeks were not easy for Chris. After being chastised by his father, he became withdrawn and refused to do any of his homework. Eventually, Louis found a local clinic that offers services for families on a sliding scale fee basis, and Chris began the testing process with the psychologist there.

A month later they had the results of the test. It appeared that Chris was a bright child but had significant issues manipulating spatial concepts. His visual memory was also weaker than his auditory (listening) memory. It was not surprising that he was having difficulties with the present math curriculum. The psychologist suggested that Chris work with a tutor who understands his learning style, and who could teach him these spatial concepts accordingly. She recommended that Chris work with one of the learning remediators who was on staff at the clinic. The psychologist also spoke with Chris's teacher and gave her some suggestions about tailoring the math program for him.

What does all of this have to do with risk-taking? When Chris experienced these academic difficulties, he shut down. In Chris's case, this was taking a poor risk because he opted to avoid working hard because he felt overwhelmed and incompetent. He told his father, "I didn't think that even working hard would make a difference. I am sick of this whole thing."

Chris was not a natural risk-taker, and this academic setback exacerbated his risk-avoidant style. In this situation Chris's inability to pay attention in class was a result of avoiding feeling even more incompetent.

Armed with this new information about Chris's learning style, Louis, Liz, Chris's teachers, and tutor all worked on a plan to support his learning and good risk-taking in school. There were ups and downs, but over time Chris's grade in math improved.

Risk-taking follows a predictable developmental trajectory in school, just as it does at home, on the playground, or in the community. As we discussed in Chapter 2, certain risk-taking behaviors are expected—indeed, necessary—to move to the next stage of development. In Chris's situation, an important first step was identifying the specific issues that were interfering with Chris's learning. But this was only the first step. It was also important to understand his learning style in the context of his evolving risk-taking style. Had Chris's parents and teachers not understood this, Chris would have been more likely to continue to avoid mastery to protect himself from the feelings of incompetence. He may have begun to take more poor risks, such as increasingly tuning out in math class and elsewhere.

TEMPERAMENT, LEARNING STYLE, AND RISK-TAKING IN SCHOOL

In Chapter 4, we discussed how different temperamental styles lend themselves to different ways of approaching risk-taking. The connection between the temperaments of both parent and child influences the evolution of emotional risk-taking. This is also true of the teacher and student.

It is a hard enough process for the parent who has one or a few children to create a strong parent-child connection. How can a teacher, who has 25–30 students in his classroom, possibly accommodate their highly divergent and evolving risk-taking needs? And how can a parent support risk-taking in the classroom for his child without being intrusive?

Before a teacher can begin to develop a program for risk-taking, he needs to understand how temperamental style and learning style affect risk-taking in a school setting.

About Temperament and Risk in School

In Chapter 4 we listed seven temperamental factors that contribute to risk-taking. We also explained that these are not absolute or static, and are best understood as occurring on a continuum. These factors and their continuum are listed again here:

- Extremely shy → Extremely outgoing
- Extremely cautious → Extremely spontaneous
- Extremely even-keeled → Extremely volatile
- Extremely self-contained → Extremely socially concerned
- Highly focused → Highly distractible
- Low energy → High energy
- Extremely adaptable → Extremely inflexible

These traits affect a child's ability to take risks in a school setting. A child who is moderately outgoing and has a moderate activity level, a moderate intensity level, high adaptability, generally positive moods, a greater tendency to approach new situations, persistence in the face of frustration, and lower distractibility will have an easier time in school. On the face of it, he will tend to be more successful in an environment that requires concentration and focus and presents learning challenges, new people, and new situations.

However, as discussed earlier, inborn temperamental traits can be modified by the child's environment. An environment that supports the strengths of the child and teaches cognitive and emotional skills optimizes the child's capabilities. In reality, though, few of us are born with exactly ideal amounts of each of these seven traits. Some of us lack the energy to persevere; yet, we can be quite adaptive. Others of us are cautious to a fault, but are very even tempered and usually in a good mood. Still others are very shy, yet are keen observers and highly adaptable.

Neither teachers nor parents can adapt a curriculum (or home environment) to match all of the temperamental needs of a specific child, nor is this necessary or helpful. Like the parent, the teacher who is familiar with the importance of risk-taking and knows her students (and herself) well enough, can usually foster an environment that develops good risk-taking. There are some predictable patterns that emerge, though, in terms of risk-taking, temperamental traits, and learning. We discuss four of these patterns here.

The Shy, Cautious Child. A highly reactive (or sensitive), shy, and cautious child will naturally tend to be reluctant to take risks. Such a child will want to hone his skills before he takes risks. Parents might notice that this is the child who makes sure that he is completely balanced before taking his first step. He is the child who might warm up slowly in a new classroom and who doesn't rush into new friendships.

In school, before he volunteers an answer in class, he will generally be quite certain he knows the correct answer. Being in the spotlight or in novel or highly stimulating situations can tend to make this child feel anxious, frightened, and overwhelmed. Therefore, this child may tend to be quiet in class, and he will not normally volunteer to be the first one to go up to the board and demonstrate a math problem.

This child may, however, be able to take academic risks at home. He may have the tenacity to struggle through difficult math problems on his own, or in the presence of a parent. Shy children are usually quiet and reserved in public, although not necessarily in a one-on-one setting. It is helpful for the teacher to contact this child's parents to find out the situations in which he shines so she can replicate them within the classroom. Parents may need to advocate for their child by initiating a call to the teacher and offering this information about their child's personality and learning style.

It can be helpful for the teacher to do some one-on-one work with the child or to speak to him privately to shore up skills. Another useful strategy is for the teacher and child to "stage" an interaction. For example, the teacher can work privately on a specific problem with the child, thereby increasing his confidence, and call him up to the board to demonstrate the problem to the class. Again, parents can suggest such interventions to their child's teacher.

Shy children need to be given small increments of risk-taking opportunities so that they have enough safety and don't feel frightened. Small increments not only help shy children feel safe, but one success builds upon another. With each success, the child can take more risks and thus can strive even further. By nature, such a child will weigh out the safety, the risks, and potential gains in any situation, and he will tend to lean toward the safety side of the equation. However, every child needs a personalized formula that will allow her to take the next step. It is important for parents and teachers to partner to do what they can to create the best academic and social risk-taking environment for that individual child. A child who is risk-avoidant as a first grader will not necessarily be the same as a high school student if, along the way, he receives the support to take the necessary risks for growth and change.

The Inflexible Child. Inflexible children can also be reluctant to take risks in school. Transition and change can be very difficult for such children, and change is an inherent part of risk-taking. To take a risk entails trying something new or doing it differently.

For the child who loves to say "no," the change that risk brings about is frightening. This child tends to want to control situations so that he feels as if he is in charge and most often the winner. When a child needs to win, he will not allow for failure. Without failure there can be little growth. This child learns to argue vociferously on almost any subject, for better or worse. For example, he articulates convincing arguments against trying a new food or about leaving the house without a coat on a cold, snowy day. Defiant children can be quite exhausting for teachers and parents.

Certain aspects of the school experience are difficult for these children. Getting along with other children, particularly when the other child wants to have some decision-making role, can be difficult. The transition from one school activity to another can be challenging because the child is still involved in the prior activity and doesn't want to move on. These children also tend toward perfectionism, and when their performance does not match their expectations, extreme frustration can result. Sometimes such children experience meltdowns when their perfectionist expectations are not met.

The Impulsive, Distractible, High-Energy Child. The impulsive, distractible, and high-energy child can also have her share of difficulties with risk-taking. This is the child who tends to take risks without necessarily thinking them through. She is the child who leaps from one high monkey bar to another and has more than her share of accidents. She may shoot her hand in the air to answer a question in class before actually knowing yet whether she knows the answer. On the playground, if she is annoyed or frustrated by another child, she may resort to pushing or hitting first rather than talking it out. The challenge for this child is in holding onto her feelings, tolerating the frustration and pressure of not knowing what to do, and thinking it through before acting.

The Low-Energy, Inattentive Child. There is also the low-energy and inattentive child. This combination of temperamental traits can also pose difficulties for positive emotional risk-taking. His effort may be spent merely moving from activity to activity, or from thought to thought, and he may not focus on the risk at hand. He may be thinking about yesterday's soccer game during class so that the information being taught has slipped right by him, rendering him unable to process it or to participate in the class discussion.

For this child, to answer a teacher's question for which he doesn't have adequate information can feel too risky. Children don't like to appear stupid, unprepared, or wrong. They don't want the teacher to reprimand them for "spacing out."

IN EVERYDAY SCHOOL LIFE temperamental differences affect classroom and schoolyard behaviors in a myriad of ways. The children described above represent some common ways that temperamental differences influence emotional risk-taking. Teachers and parents who have become familiar with the nuances of emotional risk-taking are better prepared to thoughtfully problem-solve to help their child move forward in learning good risk-taking skills. Collaboration between parents, teachers, and other educational or psychological experts can be an essential factor in managing and strengthening academic skills. It is very important for all the adults involved to be on the same page.

About Learning Style and Risk in School

A child's learning style contributes significantly to the ways in which a child approaches risk-taking in the classroom. In Chapter 2 we discussed briefly how each of us has an individual thumbprint for learning. We know that we vary in our ability to learn. For example, some of us learn vocabulary, verbal analogies, and verbal facts easily, while others are more facile with visual puzzles or pictures (also called nonverbal learning). Some of us can learn better visually than auditorily and vice versa. Additionally, some of us are faster problem solvers than others.

We also vary in *attentional abilities,* or the way in which we can attend to incoming information. Then, once we take in the information our brain has to process it; this is referred to as *processing abilities.* Finally, our brain has to store and then retrieve the information, for which we utilize our short- or long-term memory capacities. Our learning differences are determined neuropsychologically, and like our temperamental types, most of us have a combination of learning styles.

As with temperamental differences, the child who is strong across domains, can focus well, and retains both visual and verbal information fluidly is at an advantage in the classroom. This child can usually function well academically no matter what her temperamental strengths and weaknesses are.

Many children, however, have uneven learning styles. For example, a child may be an excellent reader, but he can't keep place values in mathematics straight. We have learned that children tend to avoid taking risks in the areas in which they feel weak, vulnerable, or incompetent. Like Chris in the vignette above, they tune out in such situations. This is an avoidance strategy that generally doesn't work very well. Teachers and parents need to become careful observers of their children's behaviors and to intervene promptly when a negative pattern emerges.

HANNAH AND JUDY—A SCHOOL STORY

When Hannah reached first grade, she remained a strong-willed, high-energy child who tended to want things just her way. Judy would often call her "the director," because Hannah would tell everyone just how she wanted things to be done. She wanted her food placed on the plate just so, with the pasta far away from the carrots. She ate only six different foods and would not be talked into trying anything new. She was very directive and opinionated about what pajamas she would wear. These were a few clues to how Hannah might approach school as well.

In first grade she quickly made friends she loved to run around with at recess. The other children admired her for her feistiness and physical coordination. Although she shied away from academics, nonetheless, she would look forward to going to school every day. At the first parent-teacher conference, her teacher, Ms. Asher, listed all of Hannah's strengths, among them her joy of physical activity and her joie de vivre. Yet Ms. Asher had some concerns as well.

For one thing, Hannah had difficulty transitioning from activity to activity. For example, when she was at the art table and needed to begin cleaning up for math, she would continue drawing and cutting, and would ignore reminders to finish up. When Ms. Asher approached her individually, Hannah would move her body away from her, and angrily mutter that she didn't want to go to the rug for math lesson time. Additionally, Ms. Asher observed that when they talked about number concepts, Hannah didn't readily understand and she would tune out, saying she was not interested.

Hannah also had some issues getting along with other children. During recess she would play happily with the other children until the other children did not want to play what she wanted. She would then try harder to direct them in the play, and if that didn't work, she would want to quit the game altogether.

Hannah's teacher asked Judy if she observed these behaviors at home and Judy described her directive tendencies. They forged a relationship in which they could continue to problem-solve strategies together to help Hannah's adjustment in and out of school. A few times during the year, Hannah's teacher made time to see Judy first thing in the morning, before the start of school, and sometimes they would communicate by e-mail.

One of the strategies they devised was to give Hannah a 5-minute warning before a transition and engage her in a brief dialogue about what she would need to do to finish up what she was doing. Her mother and teacher also worked collaboratively to prepare her briefly for her next activity. She was asked to respond to her mother and teacher verbally. "Yes," Hannah would say, " I know that I have 5 minutes left until reading group [or dinner] begins." This helped her understand fully what was expected of her, process it verbally, and put it into action. When she was able to transition with a minimum of opposition, she was praised and encouraged to talk about her success.

While Hannah was an adventurous and sometimes impulsive risk-taker for physical pursuits, she stuck with the familiar in school. Thus in some instances Hannah craved risk, and in others she avoided it. In terms of her approach to academic risk, Hannah gravitated to the activities that she was good at and was reluctant to move on to another that might challenge her. This reluctance precluded new experiences, and thus new academic growth.

Hannah's teacher dealt with her reluctance to engage in math time by making it more accessible, physical, and fun. She assigned her the role of "chalkboard writer," and when she demonstrated concepts with math manipulatives, she asked Hannah to hold them up for the class to see. When the class divided into small work groups, she often made her group leader. This appealed to Hannah's desire to be in charge and her natural leadership qualities. Eventually, with her strengths supported, she eased into trying activities that felt risky.

Hannah's teacher and mother problem-solved about how to help her get along well with her peers. Hannah had plenty of friends because she was fun and charismatic, but she would get into tiffs with them when she wanted things her own way. Ms. Asher talked with Hannah about her behavior on the playground in a gentle, nonintrusive way. Hannah acknowledged that it made her angry when her friends wouldn't play "fair," as she called it. They talked about how disappointing and frustrating it can be to not get to play the game you want. This discussion helped Hannah feel better understood and thus safer. A child doesn't behave in a bossy manner because she prefers it, but it is a temperamental tendency that arises when she feels a lack of control in a challenging situation.

The next step was to help her acknowledge that she really enjoys playing with her classmates, and to help motivate her to work toward this goal. Thus began a series of small steps toward helping Hannah feel comfortable and in control enough to take the risks necessary for her to loosen her tight grip on all situations.

During the first grade there were small but significant successes. For example, she accepted another girl's idea to play a game of jump rope. She also enjoyed the small-group work in math class, so she stopped avoiding math. There were still some small failures. Hannah continued to take some unsafe risks on the playground equipment, and occasionally became so angry with a friend that she would storm off the playground. Hannah and her teacher discussed both her successes and failures in a relaxed and matter-of-fact way. Slowly, she began to develop an awareness and a tolerance for the fact that some skills come easily and some are a bit harder. By the end of first grade Hannah had progressed toward taking more and more small risks that brought her closer to developing better frustration tolerance for the areas that challenged her, namely, being able to transition more easily and work through disagreements with her friends.

A GUIDE FOR DEVELOPING GOOD RISK-TAKERS IN SCHOOL

In the best of all worlds, parents and teachers work together respectfully and cooperatively to move their children and students toward positive risk-taking. Figure 5.1 summarizes the steps for parents to take in order to address risk-taking issues in school. Below we offer a teacher's guide for developing good risk-takers in school. Parents can learn from this section what constitutes a model risk-taking curriculum and can share some of these ideas with their child's teacher. There are other curricula that we also recommend, such as those that emerged from The Project for Social Emotional Learning and The Collaborative for the Advancement of Social Emotional Learning (Cohen, 1999). They offer creative strategies for promoting powerful incentives for the integration of social-emotional learning into intellectual learning.

The principles of the risk-taking curriculum are based, first and foremost, on a model of respectful collaboration. Teachers, like parents, need to familiarize themselves with the rudiments of the developmental trajectory of emotional risk-taking. It is recommended that a parent-teacher evening be devoted to talking about the importance of emotional risk-taking, and conducting risk-taking workshops for parents (and teachers) in which they can experience firsthand what it feels like to take a risk in a classroom.

For preschoolers and children in Grades 1–4, ongoing discussions about risk can be incorporated into the curriculum in different ways. Risk-taking can be discussed in and of itself, and it can also be incorporated into existing curricula. For example, with younger children, morning group meetings, at which children share their personal ideas, projects, and experiences, are ideal times to introduce the difficulties and benefits of emotional risk-taking. In older grades, health and ethics classes are ideal times to discuss emotional risk-taking, although discussions about risk-taking can also be incorporated into history, English, math, or science classes.

A MODEL CURRICULUM FOR DEVELOPING EMOTIONAL RISK-TAKING FOR 7–8-YEAR-OLDS

Ms. Henriques had a diverse and challenging group of second graders. Ms. Henriques knew from her many years of teaching that every child presents with his or her unique set of educational and emotional needs, yet there were a number of children whose issues stood out in this group. There were, for example, the three children who were already diagnosed with attentional issues. Among these children, one of them tended to be dreamy and inattentive, and two of them were overly active and impulsive. There was also a very shy boy whose family had just moved to the United States from Ecuador, so English

FIGURE 5.1. Steps for Parents to Address Risk-Taking in School

1. Know your child's temperament, learning style, and risk-taking style. You will be able to better advocate for your child in school if you can clearly articulate "who he is," his learning style, and his risk-taking style.
2. Be aware of your own temperament, personality, and risk-taking style and how it interacts with your child's. For example, if you know that you tend to be outspoken and bossy, you should learn that your child's teacher may be more receptive to comments that are phrased, "I have observed Tiffany can take risks when . . ." rather than, "There's no way Tiffany is going to answer up in class if you put her on the spot."
3. Get to know your child's teacher and her teaching and personality styles.
4. Does your child's teacher "get" who your child is and how he learns best? How do you know this?
5. Meet with your child's teacher and become a partner in the educational process and the process of developing good risk-taking in school.
6. Advocate for your child, but don't dictate to the teacher. She is the educational professional.
7. If there is a learning or behavioral problem that is not appropriately understood, consult with a professional with expertise in education.
8. Become the liaison for the teacher and outside professionals to ensure so that everyone is on the same page.
9. Remember that there will be lumps and bumps throughout your child's school experience as you guide him toward good risk-taking.

was his second language. There was another boy in her class who was physically handicapped and used a wheelchair to navigate around the classroom.

Ms. Henriques had observed since the start of the year that this was not a classroom of children who would mesh as a group easily. There were a number of intense personalities in this class, and they could easily intimidate some of the others. She decided to focus on the elements of emotional risk-taking to help gel and develop the dynamics of her class.

Working with the Parents. First, during parent orientation evening in September, she spoke to the parents about the concept of risk-taking. She summarized the central concepts presented in this book, focusing on the value of emotional risk-taking and how it grows and changes over the course of development. She told the parents that she was going to encourage all of the children to develop good risk-taking to learn, unencumbered by fear of failure, and to prevent poor risk-taking behaviors in the classroom, such as bullying, clowning around, and tuning out.

Ms. Henriques also scheduled two follow-up parent workshops on understanding the benefits of risk-taking in the classroom. In the first workshop she divided the parents into three groups according to their learning styles. In advance of the workshop, she asked the parents to describe what they feel most comfortable learning, and what types of learning most interested them. She posed a series of questions to them, including the following:

- Do you prefer learning about the humanities, mathematics, computers, natural sciences, physical sciences, and/or the arts and theater?
- Do you prefer to work/study alone or in a group?
- Do you like speaking up in groups and speaking publicly?
- Do you learn best by listening, seeing, kinesthetics (using your body), touch, or a combination of these elements? Do you use these skills in your workplace?
- What is your job or profession?

The group talked about what kinds of tasks would pose the greatest risks for them. For example, the shy computer-whiz parent offered that it would be a huge risk for her to memorize a poem and deliver it orally. The art-teacher parent said that if he had to solve an algebra problem, it would be uncomfortable and possibly embarrassing.

In the second workshop Ms. Henriques actually divided the parents into two learning experiences—one based on their strengths, and the other on their weaknesses. So the art teacher, for example, was first placed in a group in which he had to create a mural of the city, something he considers a strength. Then he was placed in a group in which he had to act on his weakness by solving math problems and demonstrate his findings to the group. After these simulated experiences they were able to talk, again, about how their temperaments and learning styles affected their risk-taking in groups.

Working with the Children. Meanwhile, in the classroom Ms. Henriques was running a parallel program for the children. She introduced the topic of risk-taking and talked about examples of both good and bad risks. She described how risk-taking happens naturally anyway, so the more we know about good risk-taking, the better. In class discussions and in the students' daily journal assignments, the children were able to voice their questions and concerns about risk-taking. For example, one girl wrote, "Ms H—This makes me feel a lot better! I thought that it was just me who gets all sweaty before talking!"

Risk-taking became a regular topic in the classroom. Small and large risks were articulated and attempted by the children. Some were successful. Some were failures. Perhaps the most heart-warming risk was when Tony, the boy in the wheelchair, said that he wanted to play basketball. In the past he had gone to physical therapy during gym time. The children—some of whom had been daunted by Tony's demands at first—applauded and supported his efforts.

There were failures, too. Ignacio, the boy from Ecuador, went home in tears after two other boys pushed him down on the playground after he bravely asked the boys to play with him for the first time. "I am taking a *big risk* this time," replied one of the boys in imitation of Ms. Henriques's voice. "You have a weird name, and I don't want to play with you!"

Despite all of her efforts, a few of the children parodied her in a negative and hurtful way. It took a lot of effort to patch up this problem. After several meetings with Ignacio and his family, the situation was partially resolved. Ignacio wasn't able to break into the boys' social groups. His academic work was fine, but he was reluctant to venture forth toward groups of boys on the playground for the rest of the year.

These were the dramatic successes and failures, but smaller good risks were taken on a daily basis. For example, Ms. Henriques paired one of the more impulsive and inattentive children, who happened to also be strong in math, with a very calm, but inattentive child, who happened to need some extra help in math. She found that the two children not only worked together well, but through this classroom grouping, they forged a new friendship.

Risk-taking became an integral part of the curriculum in all kinds of ways. Ms. Henriques designed the social studies curriculum so that the children could evaluate the kind of risks that people have taken throughout history. The children discussed the risks that the European explorers took to sail around the globe in search of new lands, and the present-day news of athletes taking steroids to improve their athletic performance. Ms. Henriques asked the class to consider the various risks and evaluate them as good or poor risks. Framing issues this way taught the children how to look at risk-taking in new ways.

One day a girl in the class spoke about a biography she read about Helen Keller and offered one of her quotations to the class: "Life is either a daring adventure or nothing." She compared Helen Keller's thought to the lessons of risk-taking that Ms. Henriques had been teaching. "If Helen Keller can see life as an adventure, then what does that mean for the rest of us who don't have the handicaps she did?" The other children listened with the gravity of her question. Ms. Henriques knew that her program was successful.

Reflections on the Curriculum. From nursery school to college, school is the hub for risk-taking. When a child feels safe and confident, then he is in a position to make good risks, risks that are thought out well and boost a child toward growth. When a child feels frightened of failure, then she will take poor risks, risks that will prevent growth.

Parents can utilize the curriculum above by discussing it at parent association meetings and introducing it to educators. Perhaps the parent association could provide a small grant toward the development of a risk-taking curriculum in your child's school.

Parents and teachers need to recognize and understand the complex web of risk-taking because they have within them the ability to teach and guide children toward developing their best selves. Not everyone is an A student or a top athlete, and that's not what we strive to develop in our children. We seek to help them love learning and go for their interests, passions, and talents—to live life as "a daring adventure."

Risk-Taking, Independent Thinking, and Tolerance Toward Others

Basic human nature is compassionate.

—*Dalai Lama*

The good risk-taker is on a developmental trajectory toward self-confidence, self-respect, and the ability to trust his own abilities. A large part of early learning is embedded in the context of relationship—with

127

parents, teachers, peers, and with oneself (learning strengths, weaknesses, and self-esteem despite frustrations and setbacks). From this vantage point, children are prepared to take necessary risks to move ahead developmentally so that they may grow to realize their fullest capabilities and sensibilities. They are also prepared to treat others with the same respect, sensitivity, and confidence that they apply toward themselves. This entails actively using their minds and their hearts to learn about other people and other cultures and to make emotionally meaningful connections with others.

Developing compassion involves taking risks: the risk to get to know someone who is different from oneself and the risk to learn about other perspectives, cultures, and opinions. Children who know how to take good risks can move past the comfort of familiarity, the limitations and the superficiality of appearance, and can think about and connect with people and ideas in novel and unprejudiced ways.

RISK-TAKING AND THE PEER GROUP

Within any school or neighborhood there are always differences among the children, for example, in race, religious background, or cultural background. Even if your child's school isn't particularly diverse in terms of ethnic or racial differences, there are always differences in values, learning styles, socioeconomic levels, and personalities. How does your child relate to and understand people who are different from him in some way? Does he seek out a broad range of friendships, or does he stick to the children who are similar to him?

Children naturally form groups in school and social settings. They do this to create a sense of belonging and identity within the larger school environment. This is a normal part of development. Many children seek out a peer group to mitigate the anxieties of being on their own in school. All children worry, to some degree, about competition or the aggressiveness of other children. The peer group offers some protection from being a target of bullies. Sometimes these groups function in a positive way, bringing together children of similar interests and values, but sometimes they function to exclude and demean others so that the members may feel less insecure. Children's groups can harbor preconceived ideas of people that mimic the stereotypes and biases of their families and the greater culture.

There are different kinds of groups: one-on-one friendships, group friendships, and cliques. Cliques, which tend to form in the upper grades of elementary school and get more pronounced in early adolescence, are formed by mutual interests and values, but also by elements of status and popularity. They tend to be made up of same-sex individuals and have implicit rules and hierarchy. As children get older, their cliques can become exclusionary, and at times cruel. Members of cliques sometimes cling to the group for security in the social structure of the peer group. When the members have pronounced insecurities or unresolved problems with anger, they can become malicious, treating both members and outsiders in mean and insensitive ways. In this social culture, stereotypes and ignorant terms abound. Descriptive terms such as *slutty, nerd, ghetto,* and *emo* (overly emotional and dramatic) are some examples. The need to reduce people to a cliché devalues them; this need usually comes from a position of fear and insecurity.

Children who are raised by their parents with sensitivity, and who have internalized good risk-taking skills (as discussed in previous chapters), can usually navigate the social world of peers with confidence and courage. It is easier for these children to resist going along with preformed and biased information about others. Children who are good risk-takers have developed the ability to see beyond superficial stereotypes and cultural prejudices. They have the courage to risk their own position in the social strata, and they can chance expressing their own convictions and feelings, even if they go against the norm.

As discussed in previous chapters, learning to socialize is easier for some children than for others. Individual differences of temperament, learning style, and life experience contribute to how a child behaves in social situations. For some children it might take more time and effort for them to take the chance to express their thoughts. Over time, and with patience, many children become secure in expressing their own thoughts and beliefs, regardless of the prevailing notions of their peers.

Dylan Speaks Up

When Dylan was in fourth grade, a new boy entered his class in the middle of the school year. This boy, Alexander, was from Russia, and his family had recently immigrated to the United States. Although he could speak English, Alexander was shy and felt awkward because it wasn't his first language and he had difficulties in understanding colloquial statements. Moreover, he didn't know the customs and social nuances of life in this new town in the United States. The teacher appointed Dylan to be Alexander's buddy. The teacher told Dylan that this would involve sitting with Alexander at lunch, helping him a little with his English, and finding ways to make his transition into the class more comfortable.

Dylan was at first very pleased and flattered to be picked by his teacher as the class ambassador. He spoke with Alexander every day before class and invited him to sit at his lunch table along with his group of friends. Dylan had known this group of boys since kindergarten and felt very comfortable with them. Toward the end of Alexander's first week at school, a friend of Dylan's began to make fun of Alexander's accent. The rest of the boys laughed along, but Dylan did not. He watched as his new friend retreated into himself, looking embarrassed and at the same time wary of the group. The same thing happened the following week, and Dylan began to feel more and more uncomfortable, yet he didn't intervene because he didn't know exactly what to say. He related to Alexander because he had had trouble expressing himself when he was younger. He, too, had worried about being teased. Dylan also was afraid to go against the group and worried that it would lead to the boys excluding him.

He decided to talk to his mom, Katie, about his problem. Katie listened to Dylan's concerns and asked him a few pointed questions. How would he feel if he was in Alexander's position? How would he feel about himself if he doesn't stand up for Alexander? What are the possible risks of acting on his conscience in this particular situation? What are the gains?

Dylan was most comfortable as a writer and so he wrote out answers to all of his mother's questions and came to a few insights:

1. Maybe his friends don't understand how they are affecting Alexander.
2. If he stands up to the ringleader, the other boys might stick up for him and they might not.
3. If they don't respect his actions to stand up for Alexander, then maybe they are not the great guys he thought they were. However, he had two friends that he hoped would be loyal friends, no matter what.

Dylan decided that if another incident occurred, he would say what was on his mind. At lunch that next day, he got his chance. The group leader harshly imitated Alexander's thick accent. Laughter followed, and this time Dylan spoke up.

> "I don't know if you realize it, dude, but you're making Alexander uncomfortable. If I were him, I'd get up and walk away from you."
>
> Tim followed with, "Hey Dylan, you becoming a Ruskie yourself?"
>
> "Just cut it out, Tim. OK?" Dylan countered.
>
> Tim looked around to the other boys, who all just sat in silence. "Whatever, dude," Tim replied in a facesaving manner.

Just then another boy joined their table and launched into a story about something funny that had happened to him on the lunch line. The tense moment had passed.

By using his skills in good risk-taking, Dylan was able to think and act in an independent manner that was consonant with his values and feelings. He used his area of cognitive strength (writing) to help him understand the problem and the potential risk, cost, and gain of standing up for his new friend. Given their ability to communicate well together, he sought out his mother for guidance. She knew her son's learning style was one in which he needed time to process his thoughts and feelings, and was careful not to push him to make a quick decision. She also had confidence he would emerge with the right ethical decision. If he had felt stuck or unable to take the smart risk, she probably would have sat down with him to rethink the problem and help him figure out the fears that were stopping him from acting on his conscience.

In this scenario a boy who was different from the others was subject to ridicule because he was different. Differences are unknowns, and unknown factors often make people uncomfortable. One defense that people use to cope with the feeling of vulnerability and uncertainty is to separate and distance themselves from it. ("Me? I don't feel uncertain, I'm cool. That kid is the uncertain one.") By bringing attention to someone else's discomfort, it averts the attention to them. Dylan was able to see past Alexander's differences and get to know him for who he was. He was able to take the social risks involved in including him with his friends and supporting him even when it meant going up against the group. For many children, this is not an easy task. Whether it be standing up for a kid who's being bullied or talking to the loner who always sits by himself at lunch, children need to be able to take the risks involved in extending themselves beyond the comfortable, safe place. The risks are real, yet the rewards in terms of self-esteem and enlargement of one's social world are great.

RISK-TAKING AND BREAKING BARRIERS

What Is Tolerance?

In her book *Teaching Tolerance: Raising Open-Minded, Empathic Children* (1996), author Sara Bullard discusses what she refers to as "habits" that predispose people to be intolerant of others. She faults human beings' tendencies to excessively categorize new information, generalize from limited evidence, prefer the familiar over the unfamiliar, rank ourselves and those around us, and to seek conformity within our social groups. Bullard points out that these tendencies can be subconscious; and while they help us make sense of the world and help us feel secure, they also lead to stereotyping and prejudice.

Bullard (1996) explains what tolerance involves and the traits it requires:

> Being tolerant means being willing to think in new ways: to withhold judgment instead of leaping to conclusions, to change our minds, to accept new information, to admit when we've made a mistake, to live with uncertainty and ambiguity. To do these things requires enormous courage, honesty, and above all, a sense of personal security—emotional resources that in many of us are frail at best. (p. 36)

Bullard goes on to point out that tolerance is learned, first off, from one's family. It can also be learned by bold self-examination and the willingness to recognize one's own shortcomings and prejudices.

Smart risk-taking is also a necessary ingredient in being tolerant toward others. We need to take the risk, intellectual and emotional, to see past our own as well as our family's and society's prejudices. Taking the risk can entail thinking about people and situations in new ways and reaching out to people who are different from us. We can reread articles in the newspaper or from our history books, taking a different perspective than we did in the past. We can ask ourselves new, different, and perhaps provocative questions about the world around us. Most often, risk-taking involves examining our relationship to others.

Can Tolerance Be Taught?

Various programs have been created to expose children of all ages to situations that challenge their hearts and minds in ways that teach them profound lessons of tolerance and compassion for others. Some of these programs are mentoring programs for children of different backgrounds, like Cookies & Dreams and Each Teach. In these mentoring programs barriers are broken through taking positive risks—by student and parent alike. Parents enroll their children in a program that will expose their child to new ways of thinking and feeling. The risks involve potential discomfort in venturing outside familiar reference points. Parents likely ask themselves, "What if my child is upset by what he learns or knows about the other child's circumstances?" "What if she develops different thoughts or opinions than I have?" "What if he has trouble remembering his lesson and ends up feeling embarrassed in front of his peers?" But through experiences in nurturing, caring, and teaching others, children from different backgrounds learn to understand one other. With understanding, compassion and tolerance emerges.

Another program, Seeds of Peace, teaches conflict mediation to children of very different and often hostile backgrounds, utilizing various fun activities and dialogues facilitated by professionals. While this program involves adolescents, parents of young children can learn a great deal from programs like this one. For one, these programs provide a long-term view of what your own child may be doing one day, and they can also be used as models for creating interesting community service programs for younger children.

Cookies & Dreams. Some years ago one of the authors teamed up with Common Cents, an organization that promotes social activism and service learning for children. The purpose was to create a cross-aged mentoring program that brings together children from vastly different socioeconomic backgrounds to help children develop relationships with each other, get past the prejudicial stereotypes, and provide an enriching learning experience for all the children. In this program, fourth, fifth, and sixth graders from a Manhattan private school, the Ethical Culture School, met weekly with preschool children from homeless shelters in the city. The preschool children came from shelters that were run by exemplary social service organizations to participate in the after-school program called Cookies & Dreams. Cookies & Dreams met once weekly throughout the school year, most often at the Ethical Culture School; approximately once a month the program was held at the day care center of the homeless shelter.

Prior to the commencement of the program, the older children (ages 9–12) were taught methods of reading to preschool children that would be fun and stimulate and engage young children. They were led in discussions about their expectations of children who were living in homeless shelters that included conditions of homelessness and the factors that lead to it. Age-appropriate discussions about preconceived ideas about homeless families were facilitated.

Big and little buddies were paired up and the program began with a reading period, where little buddies chose from an array of picture books that their big buddy would read to them. Reading was an animated and fun experience for both children and gave structure to the unfolding relationships. Then the buddies would engage in an art project that was designed to allow creative expression, learn shapes and letters, and extend the theme of the book. Next was a period of free play in the gym. Finally, all the children and mentors got together in a circle for a cookie, a song, and a final squeeze—a hand squeeze that started with one buddy pair and was sent all the way around the circle. This last activity brought the children together as a whole and functioned to give solidarity and identity to the Cookies & Dreams group.

After the buddy work was done and the younger children had left, there was a reflection time in which the mentors processed how the session went for all involved. Big buddies talked about the time spent with their little buddies and related memorable moments. They bragged about their little buddy's accomplishments and asked questions about how to better handle challenging situations that arose. Sometimes in conversations with their buddies they were told about experiences with poverty and loss that were foreign to their own. This reflection session was integral to the program in providing a forum for the mentors to talk about the differences in their lives and their buddy's life, and in giving them tools to feel empathy for these differences among them. Whatever sadness or fears they had for their buddies was balanced by the sense of empowerment they got from being an active helper.

Caring relationships inevitably formed between the mentoring pairs. Younger and older children looked forward to seeing each other each week, and were visibly disappointed if the other one was absent. Both sets of children benefited from the program by being exposed to people and experiences that were outside their everyday ones. The younger children developed a positive relationship to books and reading, were stimulated intellectually and psychologically, and made new friends. The older children deepened their capacity for compassion and learned how to nurture. All of the children learned to look past differences and see humanness.

Each Teach. Cookies & Dreams was later developed into a within-school cross-mentoring program in New York City public schools in the South Bronx. It was also redesigned by the two authors of this book to become a mentoring and tutoring program called Each Teach. Each Teach involved high school students from the Fieldston School in Riverdale, New York, and younger children with learning difficulties who were a part of an after-school music program in East Harlem. The idea of Each Teach, which was jointly sponsored by the Fieldston School and the Jewish Board of Family and Children's Services, was to have the two groups of cross-aged students teach each other. The older students who were paired up with the younger students tutored them in academic subjects, and they also helped their younger peers prepare lessons to teach to their mentors. They drew from individual areas of strength that the young boys would feel comfortable and interested in teaching such as hip-hop, rock or classical music, and sports and computers.

Teaching something to another person is a valuable way of learning the material well and deriving self-esteem from imparting one's own knowledge to another. For both the older and the younger children, teaching was a risk; in creating their lessons they each moved away from certainty as they risked the possibility of success or failure. Through the caring relationships that developed, as well as the power inherent in teaching something to another person, both groups of children helped each other.

Seeds of Peace. The internationally renowned program Seeds of Peace provides a powerful example of how older children from different parts of the world can come together and break down long-established and hostile barriers created by nations and religions. Founded in 1993 by journalist John Wallach, Seeds of Peace started as a summer camp experience set in the peaceful, pristine woods of Maine, far away from the children's war-torn homelands. Teenagers from various regions of conflict, including Israel, Palestine, Egypt, and Pakistan were brought together with teens from the United States to learn conflict mediation through fun and interactive games, sports, dialogue, and artistic activities. These teenagers bunk together, segregated only by gender. They live, play, learn, and have meals with children who are regarded as mortal enemies. Almost all the children have family and friends who have fought in their nation's armies and have died defending their side of long-standing and deeply ingrained conflicts.

The centerpiece of the program is the dialogue sessions facilitated by professional leaders. These are intense groups in which the teens are encouraged to confront their differences through talking and listening to others, to consider the other's points of view. The aim of daily dialogues is to achieve a "new threshold for tolerating ideas and understanding perspectives that were once beyond comprehension" (http://www.seedsofpeace.org).

The Seeds of Peace camp is designed to open up young minds amid an environment of safety, trust, and new challenges. The international "Seeds" are youngsters chosen by their own governments as "ambassadors" for their country. From the moment they arrive on campus, they are taking huge risks. Most of the children are 6,000 miles from home and have never seen woods, cabins, lakes, or large trees. "They sleep in bunks next to people, who they have been taught, want to annihilate them," relates Barbara Gottschalk, one of the original creators of the program and a member of the Board of Directors. "What we're doing is expanding the circle of concern. If you don't meet those people, how will you know how to be compassionate toward them?" she asks rhetorically (personal communication, July 2008).

Some campers have never been away from home and are frightened by all the lack of familiarity, so much so that a few campers want to go home. The staff, respectful of their needs, calls the families and makes tentative arrangements to book a flight home. Only rarely, though, has a camper actually boarded a plane and returned home before the program is over.

What changes for these youngsters? It is likely that they begin to feel the satisfaction that comes from tolerating new challenges and are engaged by the mastery they feel as they develop friendships amid the intensity of the camp experience. Long-held prejudices are challenged by group encounter sessions along with the fun activities they share. Forming friendships teaches them that they are all human and have more in common than they thought.

The teens come from countries that prepare them for war. The Seeds of Peace camp teaches them that peace is possible. To make this shift, the children take enormous risks—risks that are possible in this safe, yet challenging, environment.

Barbara Gottschalk related a story about a recent camper, a Pakistani girl, who returned home and was asked if she went to a peace camp or a fun camp. She replied, "It's a peace camp, but we make peace while we're having fun." As in all forms of effective education, the element of fun is essential. Teens who are in many ways still children let their guard down, along with their inhibitions, and become more open to learn when having fun.

The risks that the Seeds take when they arrive home again are substantial. They question what they've been taught to think and believe and then integrate the push and pull of this new learning into their burgeoning adolescent identities. How will others back home accept these changes? Will their new ideas and feelings create conflicts or even ostracism? This is scary stuff. Yet many of the Seeds emerge from the program as young leaders who will advance, in their own families and home communities, reconciliation and coexistence in the world.

SERVICE LEARNING PROGRAMS FOR YOUNG CHILDREN

Children as young as 3 years old can become involved in service learning projects that practice good risk-taking, and help develop compassion and empathy toward others. For preschoolers, these experiences can be simple and planned by parents. For example, creating a get-well card and then visiting a sick relative is a natural way to develop compassion. Encouraging your child to talk about her feelings after the visit helps her process and solidify the learning experience. This gives you the opportunity to answer any questions your child may have about the visit or talk together about any feelings that arose.

By ages 6 and 7, children can attend soup kitchens with their parents and help serve meals to the homeless. Children of this age can also participate (with their parents) in park cleanups or charity races geared for families. Many local social service agencies, community centers, churches, synagogues, and hospitals have programs for volunteers.

However, our own research has shown that programs for elementary-school-age children are scarcer than community service opportunities for adolescents and adults. Parents who cannot find, or are not satisfied with the programs they have found, have the option of creating their own programs. It entails some hard work, planning, and creativity, but it is also a venture that can be fun and very rewarding.

To create your own program, begin by reflecting and planning. A parent needs to find a block of time to think about the project. You can ask yourself some questions including: "Why do I want to create a program? What is it that I hope to achieve? What skills and strengths can I bring to this project?" If, for example, you are a teacher, you have expertise in working with groups of children. If you manage a small business, you have experience with budgeting and managing finances. Think about friends who may be interested in partnering with you in creating a service project. Ask yourself, "Will I be able to work with him? Do we share interests and values? Do our strengths and weaknesses complement one another?" Think about others who can be resources or consultants. Maybe your son's fourth-grade teacher would lend some time and expertise, or maybe the school principal started out her career in Teach For America (www.teachforamerica.org) and would be interested in helping out. There are often many untapped resources all around you that you aren't aware of until you look. Remember to keep good notes and lists of ideas, as well as a list of people to consult about getting your program off the ground.

As you think of ideas, consider your child's age and interests. A program for first graders will be different from one for fifth graders because the children are in different developmental stages. Perhaps your child loves animals and is passionate about animal rights. Or maybe your child is great with younger children and would want to get involved in an early reading or recreation program for preschoolers.

Give yourself at least a few months to get your program off the ground. You will need to determine what resources are available, in terms of consultants, children for the program, time, transportation, and money. Additionally, all programs need time to get the kinks out, so the first time you run it, you will need to be continually assessing how well it is going. Expect that the second incarnation of the program is usually much better than the first because experience is a great teacher. After this initial phase it is time to put these ideas to work. Figure 6.1 outlines the basic components for beginning a risk-taking program, from the beginning phases through planning, launching the program, and evaluating its success.

In order to help parents learn how to get such a program going, we share a sample experience: Judy's after-school quilting program that she created with her friend Anne when their daughters were in fifth grade.

JUDY AND ANNE GET GOING

Judy was sad that her own parents lived far away and Hannah only saw them during the holidays. She knew that it meant much to Hannah to visit her grandparents, and conversely how meaningful and gratifying it was for her parents to spend time with their granddaughter.

Since Judy taught in the public elementary school, she was aware of the quality community service programs at the local suburban high school, but lamented the lack of service programs for younger children. She knew that younger children have the capability to help others and that they can experience much satisfaction through being helpers. She also knew that experience in helping others gives children the impetus to further develop empathy and compassion. Judy was also aware that older people can sometimes feel obsolete and thrive by being offered the opportunity to share their time and life experiences with children.

After a period of reflection, Judy arrived at an idea that she hoped would meet the needs of senior citizens (who participate in the local community center) and fifth graders from her daughter's school. Judy began by keeping a journal of her ideas. She started from scratch and began to design a program that went through various drafts until she produced one that was simple, straightforward, and workable. She planned on creating an after-school program since she and Hannah are

FIGURE 6.1. Guidelines for Creating Positive Risk-Taking Programs for Children

1. Think about your interests. What kinds of activities are fun and interesting for you to create and plan? For example, do you enjoy reading, sewing, sports activities, crafts?
2. Engage your child in thinking about the program from the beginning. Even preschoolers benefit from being involved in planning a service learning project. For example, parents can say, "We are going to go to the place where Grandma lives now and do art projects with some of her friends. What do you think would be fun to do?"
3. Assess your own strengths and weaknesses and find partners and consultants who will strengthen the base of knowledge and expertise for creating and running the program. For example, engage other parents, school staff, community organizers, or clergy in the project.
4. Do some research. Look for other programs that may be similar to the one you envision. You don't have to reinvent the wheel.
5. Assess your own time constraints as well as your child's. Think small to begin.
6. Keep in mind your child's age and developmental stage; this will influence the kind of program that will be appropriate and useful for your child.
7. Once you have an initial plan and a core group of people with whom to work, hold an initial brainstorming meeting. Goals for the first meeting include:
    a. Define your project (e.g., literacy project with fourth and fifth graders reading to 4- to 5-year-olds).
    b. Define your populations (i.e., fourth and fifth graders from your child's public school; 4- to 5-year-olds from a homeless shelter).
    c. Establish a general timeline for beginning the project.
    d. Identify avenues of funding. Schools, community organizations, religious institutions, and corporations often have budgets earmarked for philanthropic causes.
    e. Assign responsibilities necessary to commence the project and set a date for the next meeting. For example, assign:
        i. Chairperson of project who coordinates and communicates with all participants
        ii. Secretary who keeps organized records of ideas and resources
        iii. Treasurer who keeps track of budget and funding
        iv. School liaison committee* (communicates with school or other hosting institution or group)
        v. Community liaison committee* (communicates with group who is invited to participate in program)
        vi. Curriculum planning committee* (plans activities, sessions, goals)
8. Hold additional planning meetings as necessary.

FIGURE 6.1. Continued.

9. Remember that you will learn by experience. The first time you run a program there will be kinks to be worked out over time. Be creative in finding new and better ways to handle the pragmatic dilemmas as you go along.

10. Make sure you have parents of the children in the program sign parental consent forms with explicit information about what they will be doing in the program.

11. Once the program begins, take notes on each session of the program. This will help you systematically improve the benefits the children are receiving from the program.

12. Notice unexpected kinds of learning experiences that occur as the children engage in the service program. Be aware of these and utilize them to grow and enrich the program for the future.

13. Conduct an objective assessment of your program halfway through the first year and again at the end of the year. Is it fulfilling its goals? If not, reassess.

14. Consider writing a manual of how to run the program so that other parents and teachers can duplicate it.

*   If you have a small working group, keep your goals modest and workable. You don't necessarily have to have a committee of people working on each component.

---

both available after school. Along the way, she asked her friend Anne, the mother of one of Hannah's good friends, if she would be interested in partnering with her in planning and executing the program.

Judy and Anne made an appointment to confer with the school principal, Mr. Silver, who was very receptive to their ideas and helped them think through some of the program details. He encouraged them to write a formal proposal for the project so that they could begin to get funding.

Next, Judy and Anne made an appointment to meet with the director of the local community center, which provides programs for the elderly. The director liked Judy's ideas and decided to partner with her and Anne to create a program with some of the seniors at his facility.

Judy and Anne then directed their attention toward raising money for the program. After creating a modest budget, they spoke with the local school board and the board of directors of the community center, both of which contributed a small stipend for the project. Additionally,

Judy and Anne held two bake-sale fundraisers at the girls' school to raise additional cash.

Thus the project began to come together. It would entail bringing a group of fifth graders to the local community center once a week after school to meet with the elderly people who had volunteered for the program. Each senior would be assigned a fifth-grade buddy, and the seniors would teach their young buddy how to sew with the aim of making a quilt. It was agreed that the quilt would be donated to be hung in the newly renovated dining room in a homeless shelter. In return for learning how to quilt, the fifth graders would teach the older person the basics of using a computer. Through this experience both the seniors and the children could share their strengths and expertise with one another.

Judy and Anne had to confirm the many details: getting children to sign up for the program, explaining the purpose of the program to the children's parents, signing permission slips, enlisting seniors, renting a minibus and driver from a transportation company, arranging snacks, and revising a final budget for the expenses of the program. Finally, Judy and Anne were ready to start the program at the beginning of the school's fall semester. They held an orientation session with the fifth graders and brainstormed a name for the program: "Technoquilt."

The program had an auspicious beginning, but then the problems came. First, an elderly person became ill and could not continue in the program. Next, two children decided that they didn't want to continue and dropped out. The following month, the bus company announced that they were raising their rates, presenting a fiscal problem for the program. One day Anne told Judy, "I am living and breathing Technoquilt! Last night I dreamed about the quilt."

Over time they figured out how to manage such pragmatic dilemmas. For example, they learned that they needed to better explain to the parents of the children about the nature of the relationship between the children and the seniors; this led to less attrition the following semester when they started with a new group. Then, along with the fifth graders, they brainstormed more fundraising ideas. The fifth graders planned a car wash event to raise the extra money that was needed.

At the end of each semester, the group created a lovely quilt to donate to a homeless shelter. The children presented it to the shelter director who thanked them for their gift of time and caring.

Why was this program a positive risk for the participants? This program put both the children and the seniors on the edge of emotional safety. Putting onself in an entirely new situation of teaching another person and forming a bond with a stranger from a different generation are not easy tasks.

Judy and Anna took a positive risk in creating this program without any particular expertise. For Judy, taking the initiative to spearhead a new initiative was a substantial risk, while Anne's disorganized style often impeded her involvement in these sorts of acitivites. Both Anna and Judy were somewhat anxious about their ability to launch this program, yet they were excited by its challenge. They both rose to the occasion, as each utilized the other's strengths and experiences.

SCIENTIFIC EXPLANATION FOR TAKING THE RISK TO CARE

Why do people seek out situations in which they need to tolerate the discomfort of the unfamiliar and take risks that develop their capacity for caring about others in new ways? One explanation is a biological one that comes from the cutting edge of neuroscience. Scientists are finding out that many aspects of empathy, compassion, and morality are hardwired into the brain. This is most likely the result of evolution since compassion helps mutual survival.

In a study from the National Institute of Neurological Disorders and Stroke (Moll et al., 2009) scientists scanned the brains of volunteers directed to think about a scenario involving donating a sum of money to a worthwhile charity or keeping it for themselves. When thinking about placing themselves in a position to put someone else's good above their own, the emotional state generated by their thoughts activated the primitive reward centers of the brain. These are the same areas that light up in response to food or sex. This and other recent studies of the primitive areas of the limbic system are guiding researchers toward the belief that the foundation of moral reasoning is empathy, and empathy has biological roots (Vedartam, 2007). This makes much sense from an evolutionary standpoint because it shows that the ability to vicariously relate with another's experience is an important leap in social behavior. If we are better able to emotionally connect, we are more likely to take care of one another. The discovery of mirror neurons—neurons that have an awareness of the feelings and actions we observe in others—have had much to teach us about the way that children imitate parents in order to learn everything from language to social skills. Mirror neurons enable us to read or intuit the emotions of others and "make emotions contagious" (Goleman, 2006). Neuroscientists' research on the role of mirror neurons helps us understand the neurological underpinnings of empathy and compassion. We can extrapolate from these findings that children who are the recipients of empathic behavior of parents and others, and who witness acts of compassion and altruism, and who are given opportunities to help others will themselves develop the capacity for generosity, empathy, and compassion.

In his book, *Spiritual Evolution: A Scientific Defense of Faith* (2008) the eminent psychiatric researcher George Vaillant describes the twofold nature of the human brain:

> Human evolution has created a brain that is really two brains: a mammalian brain that can feel and emote and cry in a Broadway theater and a Homo sapien brain that can speak, think, analyze and chart the path of Broadway as it runs diagonally across Manhattan.

Vaillant is referring to the left and right brain functions: the left hemisphere that processes details, words, and ideas, and the right hemisphere that handles music, visual images, and whole gestalts. The limbic part of the brain works with emotions. While we have learned that each part of the brain is a specialist, the entire brain works as an integrated whole. To achieve positive risk-taking, the emotional and cognitive regions of the brain function together to achieve effective communication of these complicated messages. The work that Vaillant is doing reinforces the findings of other neuroscientists (see Chapter 3). Vaillant's unique contribution is that he has found that spirituality is a uniquely human capacity and is very different from religious dogma. Spirituality is a result of the work of our unified brain, and it resides in our innate human capacity to feel love, hope, joy, and compassion.

COMPASSION IS A LEARNED BEHAVIOR

What does this all mean for parents? Certainly, the desire to learn about and understand others is not just a biological process. We are hardwired "to feel good" through the expression of empathy, but empathy is also a learned process. We learn it from our families, peer relationships, and, hopefully, from our schools and communities. There is also the potential to learn prejudice and hatred through these same environments. Those of us who have learned to think and feel independently are primed to take the necessary risks to overcome hurtful and intolerable messages. Human beings have the biological capacity for tolerance, but we need the help of our parents, teachers, and mentors to fully develop this innate capacity into a real skill.

Parents have the power to guide their children toward all sorts of learning experiences that strengthen children's capacities to think independently and to feel and display compassion for others. This chapter describes a few select programs that are dedicated to these aims; however, there are many other programs around the country and the world that are being created with similar missions. Parents and children can first work together toward making respectfulness, tolerance, and understanding a natural part of the family's home life. The next step is taking an active role in community service and service learning projects in the community at large. Engaging in these projects together helps solidify the child's positive risk-taking skills. The following chapter addresses all kinds of risk-taking activities for families to do together.

Chapter 7

PUTTING IT ALL TOGETHER: PARENT-CHILD ACTIVITIES FOR GOOD RISK-TAKING

One can never consent to creep when one feels an impulse to soar.

—*Helen Keller*

We know that risk-taking is a necessary, predictable, and inevitable part of development, and that every child has the capacity to become a good risk-taker. As parents, we have much power as we guide our children toward taking thoughtful risks. We have learned to discern the differences between good and poor risks and the important outcomes of positive risk-taking: accomplishment, resilience, perseverance, and greater capacity for tolerance and compassion.

Parents who understand the complexities of risk can help their child develop the inner strength and confidence to "go for it," even when things seem tough. In A. A. Milne's classic series, *Winnie the Pooh*, he acknowledged how daunting risk-taking can be for a child. In one of these stories young Piglet said, "It is awfully hard to be b-b-brave when you are only a Very Small Animal" (Milne, 1926/1996). As parents, we can help our children become brave.

GAMES AND ACTIVITIES TO ENCOURAGE RISK-TAKING

Over the years parents have asked us if there are specific games and activities that parents can do with their children (ages 3 to 10) to encourage positive risk-taking. Play is the natural medium of communication and learning for children. This is why teachers, therapists, and other professionals regularly use play to further children's development. Play comes naturally to children and is an instinctual way for them to explore and express thoughts and feelings.

Child therapists use play with children to help them identify problems and conflicts that are causing problems such as anxiety or depression. We are *not* encouraging parents to be therapists to their children. Not only do the play techniques that therapists use require a lot of specialized training, but parents who are therapists themselves are discouraged to use these techniques with their own children. We suggest that parents play freely with their children to facilitate open and comfortable communication, to create a playful and fun environment, and to encourage creativity and imagination.

In the pages that follow, we have developed a number of games and activities that encourage different kinds of emotional risk-taking and are geared for different age groups. Expressive play is, in our experience, underutilized. There are a myriad of ways that parents can playfully engage with their child, including storytelling, dramatic play, puppet/doll play, hide-and-seek, games, book writing and illustrating (young children can dictate their thoughts to the parent), and physical contests.

Some parents intuitively play in a relaxed and natural way with their child. For many parents, however, engaging in expressive play can feel awkward and unfamiliar; many of us, therefore, can benefit from the kind of primer, or review of play, that we are providing in this chapter.

We know that playing together is a fun way to develop positive risk-taking. This is because most young children can naturally figure out solutions to everyday issues through expressive play. For example, by creating an imaginary story about a princess who is afraid to go to ballet class, your child can "try on" and practice taking the risk while she tries on the feelings she has about it. Also, anything that involves having fun together contributes to a deeper and more affectionate parent-child relationship. And playing with your child contributes to language development, physical coordination, and a host of other good things. So, go play!

Some Basics of Play

1. Play between parent and child can happen spontaneously or it can be initiated by either of you. To have a positive and enjoyable experience, it is important that a time is chosen that works for both. If you or your child is irritable, cranky, or tired, or if the play will have to be stopped prematurely due to bedtime or other time constraints, the activity won't go as well for either participant.
2. You can put a time limit on the activity or game. Parents know how long their children can attend or focus. Usually, 3-year-olds can stay tuned in for a shorter period of time than a 4- or 5-year-old, but you and your and child are the best judges of this. As a rule of thumb, spending 20 minutes playing together is ample time.
3. Parent should aim to engage thoroughly and genuinely in the game. Find a way to get into it. Try to lose yourself in the fun as you were able to when you were young.
4. Parents must refrain from being judgmental of their children's expression or creations, and from disciplining them during this

game time. If your child becomes cranky or difficult during the game, end the game immediately and continue it at a later time.

5. Choose an activity or game that both of you enjoy. Sometimes compromise is necessary. If you simply cannot play Chutes and Ladders one more time, suggest another game that your child likes as well.

Storytelling Games and Risk-Taking

There is a very long history of storytelling as an effective means of communication and play. Older generations conveyed oral stories to the younger generation long before written alphabets were devised. Storytelling is valuable in so many ways; it is not only an effective tool for sharing values and culture, but it is an excellent vehicle for practicing expressive language skills. Furthermore, children learn about the structure of narration through storytelling. It is a highly creative endeavor.

We focus on the value of storytelling games as a shared play activity that can encourage good emotional risk-taking because, like other expessive play activities, your child can step into the risk experience through fantasy before trying it out in reality. Experience has shown that this makes the actual experience less formidable. Storytelling can be geared for just about any age, and can also be adapted to address just about any of the universal risks.

Let's begin with a storytelling activity that is suitable for a 3–4-year-old who is approaching her first separation from her caregiver (parent) to go to day care or nursery school. As discussed in previous chapters, the child risks feeling anxious and alone as she maneuvers independently in day care or school for the first time. An activity called mutual (or shared) storytelling can be quite effective for the child who is experiencing the trepidation of taking this risk. Child therapist Richard Gardner (1968) wrote about using this method for therapists to address and give expression to children's worries. We have adapted this therapeutic technique for parents to use with their children—not in a therapeutic way, but to creatively connect with their child and give him a vehicle for expressing important feelings. A description of our adaptation of shared storytelling is described below.

Aspects of Shared Storytelling

1. Ask your child if she would like to play a storytelling game together. Explain that you and she will take turns telling the story.
2. Try to keep a written account or recorded account of the story. It is not absolutely necessary to write it down or record it, as this activity can be an oral exchange, but writing it down or recording it creates a tangible account or book of the story.
3. For preschoolers, it is often helpful for the story characters to be animals rather than people, because children easily relate to and empathize with animals. Also, using animals in the story keeps the plot or reality separate from your child's own life, making it less about them and thus easier to "hear" and take in the message. You can experiment with characters and plots that your child finds exciting, interesting, or provocative; these would make a more engaging story. If your daughter is enamored with princesses, then there might be a puppy princess as the main character, but enchanted characters like kings, queens, princesses, and witches can stand on their own as characters without assigning an animal identity to them, because they are mythical, and thus not as real to a child.
4. Try not to guide the story with control or a heavy hand. However, adding in experiences that may feel risky in a positive way sets the tone and gently guides it. If the narrative does not make perfect sense, that is okay. It is okay to get silly. Use your imagination and creativity.
5. Set a time limit on the storytelling activity. Begin, for example, with taking five turns each. If you both want to continue after each has taken her turns, make a mutual determination as to how many more turns each participant wants to take. The collaborative effort between parent and child is central.
6. An important ingredient of this process is that your child feels (appropriately) powerful in creating and guiding the story line and comfortable and engaged enough to allow her feelings and ideas to flow.

Shared storytelling helped Tiffany face her fears about going to preschool for the first time. The vignette below also illustrates the genuine fun the pair had playing together.

Charles and Tiffany are talking about Tiffany's first day at pre-school. Tiffany will be beginning school in just one week. Charles and Tiffany had driven by the school earlier this afternoon, and school was definitely on Tiffany's mind.

"Daddy, I don't think I want to go to school."

"What do you mean?" asked Charles.

"I am just scared about it. And I like staying at home with you. It's fun."

"School will be fun, too," suggested Charles.

"I . . . don't think so. I am not going," said Tiffany.

Charles didn't pursue the topic any further, but after Tiffany's nap, she asked to play a game with her father.

"Hey Tiff, here's an idea, " said Charles, "Let's make up a story together. We'll take turns at it. I'll record it so we can remember it later." [Charles turned on the tape recorder.]

"You wanna start?" asked Charles.

"No. You," said Tiffany, who was never much of a risk-taker.

"Hmm . . . okay. This story is about a little puppy named Pink Puppy. She lives at home with her mom and dad in a beautiful pink dog house. It has pink and white cushions, and lots and lots and lots of dog toys. Pink Puppy's mommy and daddy dog give her yummy dog food and bones every day. [Tiffany giggled.] They play and play all day long."

"I want a turn," interrupted Tiffany.

She continued the story pretending *she* was Pink Puppy.

"I love my dog house. It has pretty pink carpeting and my mommy and daddy dog lick me all day long."

Charles continued the narrative thread by saying, "So, Pink Puppy liked being at home with her mommy and her daddy dog all day long. They played and dug for bones in the yard, and they had so much fun. One day Pink Puppy was sitting at the front window in the living room. All of the other little puppies in the neighborhood—Yellow Puppy, Orange Puppy, Striped Puppy, Purple Polka-Dotted Puppy. . . ."

"Rainbow Puppy, Circle Puppy!" Tiffany interrupted. "Go on, Dad, tell more," she said.

"Okay, one day Pink Puppy saw all of these other puppies walking to school with their mommy or daddy dogs. And Pink Puppy was sooooooooo happy to be home with her daddy doggie. She felt safe and cozy. So, she stayed at home day after day. But one beautiful sunny day, Purple Polka-Dotted Puppy came over to Pink Puppy's house to visit. She showed her a finger painting she did at school. And Pink Puppy, who loves drawing, looked and looked at the painting," said Charles.

"Okay. I will be Purple Polka-Dotted Puppy," said Tiffany. She continued in this new voice, "Oooo—it's so much fun at school! These paints are great—really squishy, squishy, squishy!"

Charles continued in Pink Puppy's voice, "Tell me more about school. Is it fun? Is it scary? Are the teachers nice? What other stuff do you do?" asked Charles.

Tiffany, who was entrenched in her new role as Purple Polka-Dotted Puppy, said, "Do you want to come with me and my mommy one day?"

"Maybe . . ." said Charles, who took the role of Pink Puppy, "I will think about it." Then Charles said, "So Tiff, let's stop here. We can continue the story another time. Let's play this game again tomorrow, okay?"

How Does this Work? Through shared storytelling, the child is able to use play to imagine what other characters feel, do, and experience. Imagining the experiences of Purple Polka-Dotted Puppy helped Pink Puppy think about her fears from a different perspective. She and Tiffany were both able to let go of her fear for a moment, and to envision the excitement of creating art (one of Tiffany's favorite things) in a classroom. Pink Puppy (and Tiffany) felt the desire to experience the fun that Purple Polka-Dotted Puppy was having at school. Furthermore, the mutuality of the shared story experience is, in itself, powerful. Charles was communicating to Tiffany that he not only had the time and the interest to create stories with her, but also that she is a powerful and competent storyteller whose contributions count just as much as his. Shared storytelling can be enchanting. The moments of sharing creative expression with one's child are priceless. Yet, it is not a magic pill. The next week when Tiffany began school, she was still not ready to take the risk to be in a classroom without her father.

"I still don't really want to go, you know. I'm still scared," she told Charles.

"I know. Just think how much fun Pink Puppy was missing, though. . . . And don't worry, I'm going to stick around near your school today. I'll make sure that I'm here, waiting outside your classroom even before school is over."

Again, in this conversation Charles was listening to Tiffany's fears, and he didn't dismiss them or minimize them. He also reassured her that he would be back to pick her up promptly.

Stories are best told over and over, since the messages, or the metaphors, take time to sink in. The story of Pink Puppy was continued as a bedtime story over the next few months, each time with slight plot twists and continued development of the main character, Pink Puppy. Tiffany began to feel that the puppies in the story were like friends. As experiences in preschool unfolded—getting used to separation, getting to know children, learning how to negotiate in play with other kids—the story grew and developed. It gave Tiffany an emotional outlet for her feelings about school and a place to work out small bumps in her development. It also served as a fun, comfortable, helpful bedtime ritual between Charles and Tiffany.

Shared Storytelling with Older Children. This technique works well with older children, too. It is essential that a parent gear story telling to his child's age and stage. With 7- to 9-year-olds, for example, using animals as protagonists may feel childish. For example, a boy who is experiencing trepidation before going away to visit grandparents or to sleep-away camp may be able to risk these feelings of unease through creating shared stories with a parent. The parent who knows that her child is interested in medieval warriors and kings may begin a story by saying, " And there was a young warrior who lived in a beautiful castle deep in the forest with his mother and father . . . ." For the girl who loves gymnastics, a story could begin with, "There was a girl named Eva who wanted so badly to become an Olympic gymnast. One day. . . ." Some children of this age are fascinated with sports stars, some with pop, hip-hop, or rock musicians, and some with computer game heroes. Stories can be about everyday people, too. Be mindful not to make the story so close to your child's personality or situation that they well feel uncomfortable and inhibit their involvement. Tailor your story to the topics, characters, and themes that will interest and engage them.

For the 6-year-old child who is struggling with risking the delay of gratification, a story about a spoiled prince, named Prince-Get-It-All, who ends up looking very silly because of all his demands, can provide a funny story that allows this boy to view his behavior from different perspectives and thus learn about himself in a safe, lighthearted way. Alternately, this same child can be brought into a shared story-telling game that is about a more sympathetic character that struggles with frustration tolerance and tries different methods of coping with his feelings through devising different plot outcomes.

Dramatic play and puppet or doll play can achieve very similar goals with children. Acting out a narrative through dramatic play or using dolls, puppets, or stuffed animals can also help children work through their fears about taking particular risks. These games are effective because through play—unlike through parental lecturing or teaching—the child is able to imagine the experience she is so worried to take. One of the wonderful aspects of childhood is that children, even 8-, 9- and 10-year-olds, can temporarily hold reality at bay and put their hearts and minds into the fantasy of play.

Story-Writing Games and Risk-Taking

Story-writing games are similar to storytelling games and other dramatic play games, but in this activity you and your child create a story together on paper. Usually you can taking turns contributing to your story. But, if handwriting is particularly arduous for your child or if your child is a preschooler, then your child can dictate the story to you. There may also be some situations in which you or your child create the entire story for the other to read.

For example, if you are going on vacation or business for a few days and your preschooler is feeling very worried about this, you can create a *Daddy Leaves and Daddy Comes Back* book. One parent made a book that included photographs of himself and of his child. The text was as follows:

> Page 1: "Daddy always goes to work at 8 a.m. and comes home at 6 p.m."
> Page 2: "Tomorrow Daddy is going on a business trip on an airplane" (with a picture of airplane).
> Page 3: "Daddy will be working in Peru for 6 days. Daddy misses Aiden while he is working and sends him a great big hug" (with a picture of a calendar and the pair hugging).
> Page 4: "Daddy will come home on another airplane on Sunday. Daddy can't wait to see Aiden when he gets home."

Such a story can be an excellent tool for young children (especially 3- to 4-year-olds) who are experiencing anxiety about their parents going away. Aiden and his father read this together before his dad left, and his grandmother, who was taking care of him, read it to him while his dad was away. The book now has a special place on Aiden's bookshelf.

Alternatively, you can write the story together or illustrate it together. Even if your child only helps color in the pictures, her part in creating the book can help her absorb the book's theme. These books reassure your child that mommy (or daddy) is safe and happy—and misses her. You can also include some activities, such as puzzles or drawing activities, to further engage your young child in the book.

For an 8-, 9-, or 10-year-old who is having social difficulties, creating written stories can be an effective tool. We revisit Hannah and Judy as they create a story together.

JUDY AND HANNAH'S STORY

Hannah was enjoying fourth grade immensely. She had a wonderful teacher who understood her strengths and challenges and even enjoyed her feisty and spirited ways. Hannah especially enjoyed the mathematics program that complemented her visual-spatial strengths. Hannah's teacher, Mr. Russo, encouraged his students to invent their own ways of solving problems. Encouraged to take these intellectual risks, Hannah quickly began taking a leadership role in class. Occasionally, though, her forthright and energetic manner was misinterpreted by some of the other children. They began to call her "bossy," and refused to play with her on the playground.

Judy and Mr. Russo spoke about how Hannah's risk-taking style was working both to her advantage and disadvantage in the classroom, and about the strategies he was implementing to help Hannah learn to take more measured and acceptable social risks. On her end, Judy decided to begin an ongoing writing/journal activity to help Hannah at home.

Hannah had already spoken to Judy about how a few of the other girls were being mean to her. Judy suggested that they use a writing activity to help Hannah better understand her role in these interactions. Since Hannah was almost 10 years old, they decided together that rather than create a fictional story, they would begin with a real situation, and then alternatively create new solutions to the problem. (This activity also helped Hannah practice writing fluency.)

One day after school Judy noticed that Hannah was in a bad mood. This wasn't difficult to figure out as Hannah was being grouchy and giving one-word answers to Judy's questions about her day in school. Judy didn't comment on her daughter's sour mood but suggested they play the writing game. "You start, Hannah. Write about a difficult situation you've had in school."

Hannah was up for the game. She sat down at the kitchen table and wrote: "Today in class, Mr. R asked me to demonstrate a math problem on the blackboard. I came up with a cool way to solve the problem and Mr. R said I did a great job. But when I walked back to my seat I saw Meredith whispering something to Kylie and pointing to me, and they both laughed. I felt like screaming at them at the top of my lungs, but I know how I am supposed to CONTROL MY IMPULSIVITY." She wrote this last part in capitals, to let her mom know that she was imitating how her mother spoke.

"I'm glad that you used self-control," Judy responded with a note of humor, after reading what Hannah wrote.

"Okay, now we each write down two ideas about what I should have done after that. Then I'll tell you what I *really did*," said Hannah teasingly.

After about 10 minutes of writing, they showed one another their responses. Hannah wrote, "So I waited until recess, and I went up to Meredith and Kylie and said, 'I hate you. You are so stupid. Why were you laughing at me? I never want to be your friend!'"

"Just joking, Mom!" said Hannah. "Now, you tell me yours."

Judy wrote, "I waited until after school, and until Meredith was alone, and said, 'You know, what you did today was very hurtful to me. We are too old to be doing these mean things. Please try to be more kind.'"

"Eww! That is so dorky!"

"How about this one?" Judy asked. "I saw Meredith and Kylie together after school. 'What was so funny during math class? You know, it's not so easy for me to demonstrate these math problems. You could be a little nicer.'"

"A little better," said Hannah. "So this is what I really said. 'You two are n-a-s-t-y!' And I walked away."

Judy laughed at her daughter's moxie.

"It was okay, but Mom, I really think that they were mad at me because I was a little bossy with them the day before . . . and I was showing off a bit."

"That's very insightful of you, Hannah. Although they should not have treated you that way, sometimes being bossy ticks people off. It's something to keep in mind next time."

"I guess . . . ." Hannah mused.

How Does This Work? This shared writing activity between Judy and Hannah is another example of using play to encourage good risk taking. Judy and Hannah were used to talking about risk-taking, and they know that Hannah has lots of risk-taking strengths, but her impulsivity could also lead her to take poor risks. In this case, the obvious pleasure she took in her new leadership role in the classroom incited some envy among the other girls. It was Hannah's natural inclination to rise to anger, show off a bit, and impulsively dismiss others' reactions. Through the writing activity, Hannah was able to slow down and contemplate her actions. It gave her an opportunity—without judgment from her mother—to think things through. She was able to analyze her reactions and to think about how she could possibly react, and interact, more reasonably and be less "bossy."

Physical Games and Risk-Taking

Some children and parents enjoy the challenge of physical activities and games. Activities such as relay races, ball games, tag, and hide-and-seek can be played to promote good risk-taking at any age. Babies aged 9 months to a year particularly enjoy the game of peek-a-boo. This is not surprising since at this age a child is beginning to experience herself as psychologically separate from her parent for the first time (Mahler, Pine, & Bergman, 1975). The game of peek-a boo, which is played over and over in a repetitive fashion, stimulates the child's sense of growing awareness that mommy can be there and then not be there, and this means she and the baby are separate entities. Likewise, large motor activities such as hide-and-seek reinforce the child's experience that he—and his parent—can hide (go away) and come back. Creating ball games or relay races not only encourages creative thinking and helps develop coordination, but children can be challenged to risk small failures as they try to master the game or race.

As Chris got older and Louis learned not to push him into sports, but rather to respect his son's own desires and talents, Chris began to want to play physical games with his Dad. He, like many of his friends, began to like the challenge of sports. When Chris was 9 years old, he asked his Dad to play soccer. Liz (gently) reminded Louis not to get overly excited about their son's interest, but to let Chris take the lead. Of course, it pleased Louis to be playing sports with his son, and thanks to Liz's reminder, he tried to play down his excitement because of their history of clashing over physical activities.

Louis was careful not to criticize Chris's inexperienced attempt at maneuvering the soccer ball. He played gently with Chris, allowing Chris to take more risks with his body and to feel a little more competent with the ball. At one point, Chris tripped as he was running, and scraped his shin. Instead of his typical, "Shake it off, son," Louis gently asked if Chris was in pain and suggested they go inside to clean up the cut. After the cut was cared for, Louis didn't suggest going back out to play, but instead said, "Sorry you hurt yourself, Chris, but the rest was fun. I had a good time."

Chris responded, "Oh, I'm okay, Dad. Let's play again."

Both father and son felt gratified about the game, as they both not only had a lot of fun, but also had been able to play sports together for the first time. Chris felt empowered by his father's respectful approach and didn't feel badly about his lack of athletic ability, as he had in the past. Chris learned to take some small risks engaging in a sport that he might eventually want to play with his friends at school.

How Does This Work? It is a powerful and inherently fun experience for parent and child to interact physically. Children love to move as they develop their gross motor skills, and also respond to the challenge of physical games. Particularly for the child who is fearful of taking physical risks, playing physical games and sports with a parent is an effective and safe way of mastering physical skills and practicing techniques that can eventually be used when playing with other children.

In Chris and Louis's situation, Louis became more knowledgeable about his son through their successful soccer play. He then came up with the idea that the two of them could tackle a new sport together: rollerblading. Louis had never learned to roller skate as a youngster, and Chris showed interest in learning. For Chris's next birthday, Louis bought Chris and himself roller blades (and elbow and knee pads), and they learned together. Each weekend they went out to the nearby park and practiced. In this instance, Chris had a faster, steeper learning curve and was soon better than his Dad. It was a great experience for Chris to excel at a sport, and he became the more competent skater of the two. This was a valuable risk-taking experience for both father and son.

Sometimes, taking up a new sport together contains the right ingredients for a fun and effective experience at good physical risk-taking. The parent and child start off on the same level, and the child can teach and cheer on his parent. This goes a long way in supporting a child's confidence, and it reinforces his ability to take more good risks as he develops.

Drawing Games and Risk-Taking

Sitting down with your child, whether at a table at home, on a picnic blanket in the park, or even on the steps of the museum is another wonderful way to share a safe, thoughtful risk-taking experience. "Why in the world would drawing together constitute a risk?" we have been asked. This is because some children are not facile with fine and grapho-motor skills, and they are reticent to use and develop these abilities. For some children, perhaps this is because their fine motor skills are a little slower to develop, or maybe they see other children at school who they believe draw better than they do. Or maybe when they do draw and color with a parent, they compare their abilities to their parent's and feel less competent. Despite the fact that children can feel inadequate in this domain, drawing and coloring is a great way to express feelings and ideas, regardless of one's talent. Spending time with your preschool or elementary school child drawing together, quietly working side by side and talking about whatever thoughts come up, is a wonderful way to spend rich, quality time together. It is also a perfect activity to encourage positive risk-taking for your child.

KATIE AND DYLAN'S STORY

When Dylan was in preschool, Katie loved to spend quiet time with Dylan drawing and coloring. At first, when Dylan was still feeling insecure about his language abilities, Katie thought that drawing together would be a great way to connect with Dylan and build his confidence. During quiet art time together, Dylan often expressed some of his worries about school and measuring up to the other kids.

One game that Katie played with Dylan was called "squiggling together." Katie's game is based on The Squiggle Game that was developed by psychoanalyst and pediatrician, D. W. Winnicott (1975). Winnicott used this game as a technique for understanding a child's unconscious thoughts and worries. Katie used this game to encourage Dylan to try out new artistic skills, thereby increasing his confidence in this domain. Katie would draw a spontaneous squiggle on a blank piece of paper and Dylan was to make the next squiggle. They would take turns and finally see what kind of design emerged. They would then color it in together. At first, Dylan needed to be coaxed into participating, but when he realized there were no perfect squiggles, and that neither exact words nor perfect squiggles mattered, he quickly took to the game. From this vantage point, he began to practice shapes and, later on, letters.

One day when Katie and Dylan were drawing together, Dylan said, "Emily, in my class, can draw a person, and I can't."

"Do you want to try, Dylan?"

"I can't," responded Dylan.

"You never know if you don't try," Katie said. "First we each draw a circle." Dylan drew a circle he had done many times in the squiggle game. "Now, we need some eyes, right? Do you want to draw two dots or two little circles in the circle?"

"Two dots," Dylan said quietly.

"OK, what comes next?" Katie asked.

"A mouth!" Dylan said more loudly and with enthusiasm. He then drew a crooked but discernable line for a mouth.

"Oh my gosh, this is looking like a person's face!" Without saying anything, Dylan then drew two lines coming out of the head that represented the person's legs. "We're on a roll," Katie said conspiratorially, and they both giggled. And so Dylan learned that he too could draw a person on his own. After several more play and drawing sessions with his mom, Dylan took the risk of sitting down at the drawing table at school, and, along with Emily and the other children, drew pictures with people in them.

How does this work? Art is an effective, nonverbal means of expression. Art therapists utilize their patient's deep-seated and sometimes primitive feelings, thoughts, and ideas and help the person channel them through the therapeutic vehicle of art. In fact, art therapy is particularly helpful with post-traumatic stress disorder because traumatic memories are frozen in time in the neurological circuitry of the right brain—the nonlogical, nonlanguage part of the brain. The expression of feelings through art helps people understand their worries first in a nonlinguistic way, and later through words, to further the understanding. Various art forms, including visual art, dance, and music, can be simply restorative without utilizing special therapeutic techniques. In the vignette above, Katie's squiggle game illustrates how parents can encourage artistic expression—without therapizing—to encourage risk-taking.

One benefit of playing these games with our children when they are young is that they will tend to become more emotionally expressive when they get older. They tend to replicate these activities alone, or with friends. For example, a young woman who is a dancer said, "Creating my dances can be so intimidating. Other dancers and teachers can really zap my confidence. Whenever I feel particularly frustrated, I just go into my room as I did when I was a little girl, turn on the music and move. Sometimes this turns into something that I use for a production, and sometimes it doesn't. But this always makes me feel better because I regain a realistic perspective about who I am as an artist."

In using expressive arts as a vehicle for a parent-child experience, you can simply sit down with your child to have fun making art (or playing music or dancing) together. This allows your child to be creative and express feelings that could feel risky. Having some alone time together creates a safe environment in which your child can, if he wants, talk spontaneously with you. As a parent, your job is to simply listen, not to judge or even give advice. This is a time and place to further hone the listening skills discussed in Chapter 3.

Singing Games and Risk-Taking

Singing games are also a good way to have fun, develop intimacy, and promote good risk-taking. Singing games can be silly and fun, and they develop expressive language facility in a nonacademic setting. Our experience indicates that parents, once they get the hang of this, like singing games as much or more than the children. The process is easy.

Start out using the tune of a traditional or popular song, be it "Take Me Out To The Ball Game," "Yankee Doodle," or "Puff the Magic Dragon." Then create an original first line, and hand it over to your child for a second line. If your child is reticent to contribute, do a few lines with a theme that you know will engage your child. The mother of a 4-year-old girl named Lilly explained the idea of the game to her daughter who loves music, and sang to the tune of "Twinkle, Twinkle, Little Star."

"Lilly loves to play and sing, she could perform for the best of kings," sang her mother. Lilly was immediately drawn to the song, of course, because it was about her. At first she told her mom to continue. "One day she had a little cold, and she blew her nose so bold."

Lilly laughed and then sang, "But she became a big, big star, and was on TV." Lilly stopped, looking for the next few lines.

Her mom waited and then sang "near and far." Lilly laughed.

Lilly learned how to play the game better and better over time. Learning how to word-find and rhyme are good language skills that enhance language development. Learning to take the small risks involved in sounding silly feels okay because this is a part of the game.

Building Games and Risk-Taking

Building games are another way to promote risk–taking that involves visual-spatial and visual–motor skill development. Playing with building blocks is an imaginative game that children enjoy from toddlerhood through early elementary years. There are many ways that these games can be used to encourage risk-taking. For example, a timid child can be encouraged to play a building game in which she and her parent take turns seeing who can build the highest tower without toppling it over. With a child who has perfectionist tendencies that lead to frustration, a parent and child can build a high tower, and then when it tumbles down, the parent makes that a fun, inevitable element of the game. This reinforces to the child that they're not striving to build the *perfect* tower, but to build and have fun when it's built and when it falls down. Building blocks can also be used to create imaginary towns, villages, and other settings. As with other types of imaginative play, stories can be interwoven into the block play to create scenarios to practice risk-taking.

We have found that once parents and children enjoy these risk-taking games together, they begin to create their own games and variations of the games we have described. Katie wrote in one of her journal entries, "I wish that I had been allowed to play more when I was a child. This is fun!"

DOING COMMUNITY SERVICE AS A FAMILY ACTIVITY

As described in Chapter 6, doing community service as a family, is an excellent way to help our children develop compassion and learn about philanthropy, while teaching them to think out of the box.

We have already described the powerful effects of taking the risks entailed in stepping out of the comfortable territory of one's same ethnic, socioeconomic, racial, or political community and venturing out to help others. Families can get involved with community service projects together. This way parents are modeling good risk-taking in the form of compassionate behavior toward others. Additionally, children are being provided with opportunities to do their part to help others. When a parent and child walk down the street and encounter a homeless person, children naturally ask about this. From the preschooler's question of, "Why doesn't this man have a home?" to "Can we take him home with us?" to the elementary school child's questions of "How can this happen to someone—don't they have a family to care for them?" and "What can we do to help?" children wonder about and are predisposed to care about those who are less fortunate.

Children who feel comfortable enough at a young age to ask their parents about the unfortunate situations they see and encounter are asking for an explanation to help them understand the world they live in. Skimming over or stifling such questions teaches children that the problems of the world don't have to concern them. This is not a good message to give if one is interested in contributing to a better world and raising children who will become problem solvers and positive risk-takers.

In Chapter 6, we discussed some options for doing community service together, such as working at a soup kitchen. These and other experiences stimulate questions and discussions to be addressed at home. Parents can answer simply and frankly, taking into consideration the child's age and developmental stage. Again, the practice of listening is key here.

Other community service experiences, such as delivering meals to homebound elderly people, are humane, safe, positive risks for families who are seeking to be helpful to others and be a part of the betterment of our society. Children may be timid at first in coming into an old or infirm person's home and talking to them, and parents must be careful not to push their child in any way. Just through bringing the child with them as they deliver meals, parents model compassion as they engage in a conversation with the homebound person. Children take it all in and are learning a great deal about the responsibilities that people have to each other.

We have found that children who begin service learning as young children tend to feel the competence that comes from helping others. For example, every summer Tiffany decided to hold a bake sale and lemonade stand at the local pool and recreation center with the help of her parents, to benefit the animal humane society. Tiffany, who loved animals, asked her parents if she could do this when she was just 7 years old! Charles checked with the recreation center personnel to get their permission, and this soon became an annual event.

From participating in community book sales to benefit the local library to collecting pennies, nickels, and dimes to give to the local children's hospital, engaging in community service with your child generates a powerful mechanism for enriching the parent-child relationship while teaching your child to take good, thoughtful risks. The activities described in this chapter can give your children opportunities to be thoughtful, courageous doers—people who contribute rather than take, who solve problems rather than feel victimized. This is the blueprint for teaching your child to soar in life.

PUTTING IT ALL TOGETHER

We are living through uncertain times. It is hard to know how to protect our children from danger, disappointment, and failure. Unwittingly, we can discourage them to take on new challenges. We caution our children about preparedness and safety. Along with the elementary schools, we educate young children about the dangers of predators and the use of recreational drugs and cigarettes. This education is very important—it is an essential part of knowledge about the world around us and how to stay healthy and safe. When children are knowledgeable about the realities around them, they are better able to react thoughtfully when faced with difficult choices.

Yet, there is an upside to risk. Louisa May Alcott, the author of the classic novel *Little Women*, said it so well: "I'm not afraid of storms, for I'm learning how to sail my ship." Life does contain its share of storms and the best we can do as parents and educators is to help our children learn how to be great sailors, people who can navigate in any weather. We must teach them how to assess the winds and climate, both before setting out and throughout the voyage. This is accomplished by understanding not only the dangers, but also the opportunities of risk.

Our metaphor, "Children Who Soar," is one of flying, of elevating oneself above and beyond the well-trodden terrain. Everyone has had dreams of flying. These dreams are about feeling strong, competent, and unencumbered to be able to take flight and ascend like a bird. Dreams of flying symbolize our desire to lift ourselves beyond our current circumstance, and break free of the weight of gravity, free of the limitations of our selves and our situations. They are about the pleasures inherent in accomplishment and movement upward and onward. In this book we have sought to help parents guide children toward flight by focusing on self-reflection through contemplation of their own experiences from childhood to the present, creating a strong platform from which their children can "take the leap" safely. This analysis puts them in a better position to understand their child—his unique temperament and biological endowment, learning style, life experiences, environment, and the myriad of factors that affect him over time.

We have also learned that the practice of listening facilitates this understanding. This requires actively listening to all levels of what the child is telling us, not just his words. We also know that our brain, body, and emotions are inextricably intertwined, and that by guiding children to take on new and positive behaviors and feelings, the child's neural pathways are being created and strengthened. This increases the likelihood of such further behavioral and emotional development.

Risk is a necessary part of the forward movement of development that leads to exploration, discovery, and the creation of new dreams. Moving backwards, or remaining static, is the antithesis of growth. Risk propels us to move beyond our comfort zones, past fear and complacence. We hope that parents will use this book and its practices as they guide their children to leap and soar beyond life's inevitable obstacles.

SUGGESTED READINGS

We have chosen some of our favorite books for further reading on the topics of parenting, child development, and risk-taking. Additionally, we include a short list of much loved children's books that can be read with your child to stimulate conversations about risk-taking.

Books For Parents

Bullard, S. (1996). *Teaching tolerance: Raising open-minded empathetic children.* New York: Doubleday.

> Writing from her experience working at the Southern Poverty Law Center, Sandra Bullard helps her readers confront the prejudice that is in us all, and outlines the work of overcoming narrow-minded thinking to promote a society of tolerance.

Calkins-McCormick, L., & Bellino, L. (1997). *Raising lifelong learners: A parent's guide.* Cambridge, MA: Perseus Books.

> Renowned educator Lucy Calkins shares her warmth and wisdom with parents as she discusses important aspects of raising children who are curious and happy lifetime learners. The appendices in this book are terrific and include information such as how to form a partnership with your child's teacher.

Cohen, J. (Ed.) (1999). *Educating minds and hearts: Social emotional learning and the passage into adolescence.* New York: Teachers College Press.

> Cohen's book, geared for parents and professionals, discusses the importance and the benefits of bringing social and emotional learning to the classroom. This book also includes detailed descriptions of school programs he and other educators have developed and implemented.

Corkille-Briggs, D. (1970). *Your child's self-esteem. Step-by-step guidelines for rais-ing responsible, productive, happy children.* Garden City, NY: Doubleday.
  Corkille-Briggs discusses the journey toward raising children who are confident, competent and respectful. She provides helpful checklists for parents.

Doidge, N. (2007). *The brain that changes itself: Stories of personal triumph from the frontiers of brain science.* New York: Penguin.
  In approachable language, and with some humor, Doige discusses cutting-edge research about the flexibility of the human brain. His stories reflect individuals who have overcome a wide range of challenges across the life span.

Erikson, E. H. (1950). *Childhood and society.* New York: W.W. Norton.
  A classic tome by psychologist Erik Erikson, this volume is filled with his warmth and empathy as a clinician. His psychosocial developmental model, from birth through old age, remains solid and helpful in the twenty-first century.

Ginott, H. G. (1965). *Between parent and child.* New York: Macmillan.
  Dr. Ginnott wrote about the importance of listening to your child as an important building block of the parent-child relationship.

Goleman, D. (1995). *Emotional intelligence: Why it can matter more than IQ.* New York: Bantam Books.
  Goleman, who was originally a science writer for the *New York Times,* com-bined Howard Gardner's seminal work on multiple intelligences with recent scientific research to create a new and enlarged understanding of intelligence. A groundbreaking book.

Greenspan, S., & Salmon, J. (1995). *The challenging child: Understanding, raising, and enjoying the five "difficult" types of children.* Cambridge, MA: Perseus.
  Dr. Greenspan writes for parents to help them understand and learn prag-matic strategies for raising children who can be challenging.

LeDoux, J. (1996). *The emotional brain: The mysterious underpinnings of emotional life.* New York: Simon & Schuster.
  An accessible and articulate explanation of how the intricate mechanisms of the human brain underlie the range of our emotions, including love, anger, and anxiety. This is a must-read for anyone looking to understand the neuroscience of emotions.

Levine, M. (1992). *All kinds of minds.* Cambridge, MA: Educators Publishing.
  A sensitive and informative book written for parents and children to read

together. It profiles different children with various learning strengths and weaknesses, and helps the reader understand that there are many kinds of learning styles.

Levy-Warren, M. H. (1996). *The adolescent journey: Development, identity, formation, and psychotherapy.* Northvale, NJ: J. Aronson.
While this book is written for clinicians, its reader friendly style makes it an important and informative volume for parents of adolescents—or for parents who will have adolescents one day.

Mahler, M. S., Pine, F., & Bergman, A. (1975). *The psychological birth of the human infant: Symbiosis and individuation.* New York: Basic Books.
A classic book for professionals and interested parents on the infant's psychological development and the integral relationship between parent and child.

Mogel, W. (2001). *The blessing of a skinned knee: Using Jewish teachings to raise self-reliant children.* New York: Penguin Books.
Combining the wisdom of Jewish teachings with her experience as a clinical psychologist, Mogel teaches parents how to raise self-reliant, moral, and empathic children.

Siegel, D. J. (1999). *The developing mind: How relationships and the brain interact to shape who we are.* New York: Guilford Press.
This important book synthesizes neurobiological research and child development.

Siegel, D. J., & Hartzell, M.(2003). *Parenting from the inside out: How a deeper self-understanding can help you raise children who thrive.* New York: P. Tarcher/Putnam.
Daniel Siegel and Mary Hartzell provide a parent-friendly guide to self-reflective, thoughtful parenting that emanates from a synthesis of early childhood education, psychiatry, and neurobiology.

Stern, D. N. (1985). *The interpersonal world of the infant: A view from psychoanalysis and developmental psychology.* New York: Basic Books.
Daniel Stern's book describes the rich and interactive world between parent and child from the very beginning of the infant's life.

Turecki, S. (1985). *The difficult child.* New York: Bantam Books.
Tureki's important book helps parents understand and cope with their children who are difficult to manage. Many practical strategies are included.

Children's Books

Blegvad, L. (1987). *Anna banana and me* (E. Blegvad, Illus.). New York: Aladdin.
In this picture book a feisty, fearless Anna helps out a timid boy. (Ages 3–6)

Burton, V. L. (1937). *Choo choo.* New York: Houghton Mifflin.
Choo Choo the locomotive tires of pulling grains and decides to go it alone. Although her plan is risky, Choo Choo learns that there will be others around to help should the plan backfire. (Ages 4–8)

Cannon, J. (1993). *Stellaluna.* New York: Harcourt Children's Books.
When Stellaluna, a baby bat, is separated from her mother, she winds up in a nest of birds, where she learns two important lessons: to accept the differences in others and to be comfortable in your own skin. (Ages 4–8)

Cleary, B. (1995). *Ramona the brave* (A. Tiegreen, Illus.). New York: Avon Books. (Original published in 1975)
Ramona Quimby has so many new challenges: She turns 6, she enters the first grade, she gets her own bedroom, and her mom has a new job. A story of how children face risks in just the ordinary steps of growing up. (Ages 5–9)

Cohen, B. (1983). *Molly's Pilgrim* (D. M. Duffy, Illus.). New York: Lothrop, Lee, & Shephard.
Molly, a Jewish immigrant from Russia, confronts teasing and bullying from her fellow students. By the end of the story she and her classmates learn the true meaning of Thanksgiving. (Ages 7–10)

Dahl, R. (1988). *Matilda* (Q. Blake, Illus.). New York: Penguin Books.
Roald Dahl's beloved story tells how a precocious and capable girl navigates through the difficulties of life helped by her magical powers. (Ages 6–10)

Dalgliesh, A. (1954). *The courage of Sarah Noble* (L. Weisgard, Illus.). New York: Atheneum Books for Young Readers.
This is the true story of an 8-year-old girl who goes with her father to build a new home in the Connecticut wilderness and learns to trust herself and her Indian neighbors. (Ages 7–10)

Danneberg, J. (2000). *First day jitters* (J. Love, Illus.). Watertown, MA: Charlesbridge Publishing.
Sarah Hartwell is so nervous about her first day at a new school, she can barely get out of bed. In this story, it it turns out that Sarah is the teacher. Children learn that even adults have to be brave and take risks when they start something new. (Ages 5–9)

DiCamillo, K. (2006) *The miraculous journey of Edward Tulane* (B. Ibatoulline, Illus.). Cambridge, Massachusetts: Candlewick Press.
DiCamillo tells about the wonderful journey of Edward Tulane, a stuffed rabbit who, after many disappointments, takes the risk to love again. (Ages 8–12)

Flack, M. (1933). *The story about Ping* (K. Wiese, Illus.). New York: Viking.
In this charming story both a duck and a little boy take important risks. (Ages 4–7)

Henkes, K. (2006). *Lilly's big day*. New York: Greenwillow Books.
A girl feels bad after someone else gets the role she wanted as flower girl, but when the other girl freezes up, Lilly takes over and helps. (Ages 4–8)

Lionni, L. (1963). *Swimmy*. New York: Knopf Books for Young Readers.
Swimmy, the lone black fish in a school of small, red fish, takes the risk to save the others from much bigger fish. (Ages 4–8)

Lowry, L. (1989). *Number the stars*. New York: Bantam Doubleday Dell Books for Young Readers.
Set in Denmark during the Nazi occupation of World War II, a Danish family takes in their daughter's best friend, who is Jewish. Both girls and their families show remarkable courage and take dangerous, but necessary, risks to survive. (Ages 9–13)

Martin, B., Jr., Archambault, J. (1989). *Chicka chicka boom boom* (L. Ehlert, Illus.). (1989). New York: Simon & Schuster Books for Young Readers.
Naughty alphabet letters get in trouble as they dare one another. Is this a bad risk? Can the adults in their lives step in to stop the naughtiness? (Ages 3–7)

Naylor, P. R. (1991). *Shiloh* (B. Moser, Illus.). New York: Simon & Schuster.
Acclaimed children's book author Phyllis Reynolds Naylor's classic story about an 11-year-old boy who rescues a dog from his abusive owner. The boy risks defying his parents in order to save the dog he loves. (Ages 6–10)

O'Neil, A. (2002). *The recess queen* (L. Huliska-Beith, Illus.). New York: Scholastic Press.
Katie Sue, the new girl at school, takes the risk of challenging Mean Jean, the school bully, by inviting her to play. (Ages 4–8)

Pinkney, B. (1998). *JoJo's flying sidekick*. New York: Aladdin Paperbacks.
JoJo risks uncertainty and failure as her family and friends support her efforts to advance to a yellow belt in Tae Kwon Do. (Ages 4–8).

Pinkwater, D. M. (1977). *Big orange splot.* New York: Scholastic Incorporated.
A man takes the risky step of defying the rules for painting his house in a conformist community. (Ages 4–8)

Piper, W. (1930). *The little engine that could* (D. Hauman & G. Hauman, Illus.). New York: Platt & Munk.
In this classic tale, the little engine climbs the big mountain to get the toys to the children in the valley. The risks to achieve, to persevere, and to help others are exemplified. (All ages)

Polacco, P. (1998). *Thank you, Mr. Falker.* New York: Philomel Books.
A teacher helps a girl overcome her learning disabilities. (Ages 7–10)

Potter, B. (1902). *The Tale of Peter Rabbit.* London: Frederick Warne.
A classic tale of how mischievous Peter Rabbit took a dangerous risk. (Ages 4–8)

Sendak, M. (1963). *Where the wild things are.* New York: HarperCollins.
Maurice Sendak's vivid images make this story about a young boy's wild and daring imagination come alive. This story allows children to know that their intense feelings—of anger, power, or adventure—are normal. (Ages 3–6)

Seuss, Dr. (1960). *Green eggs and ham.* New York: Random House.
In this humorous beginning reader, Sam persuades his friend to take the risk of trying a new food. (Ages 3–8)

Seuss, Dr. (1990). *Oh, the places you'll go.* New York: Random House.
A quintessential Dr. Seuss poem that teaches children to confidently trust their instincts, while using their minds and hearts through the long and winding road of life. (All ages)

Seuss, Dr. (1958). *Yertle the turtle and other stories.* New York: Random House.
One small turtle takes a risk and questions authority, freeing all the turtles from an unfair master. (All ages)

Silverstein, S. (1964). *The giving tree.* New York: HarperCollins.
Talented children's author and poet Shel Silverstein uses the relationship of a boy and a tree as a metaphor for the love and sacrifice of a parent for his child. A very moving story that teaches children about empathy. (All ages)

Steig, W. (1986). *Brave Irene.* New York: Farrar, Straus, Giroux.
A girl bravely offers to deliver a dress for her mother the seamstress, who is ill. (Ages 4–8)

Viorst, J. (1987). *Alexander and the terrible, no good, very bad day* (R. Cruz, Illus.). New York: Aladdin Paperbacks.
> Prolific children's book author Judith Viorst lets children know that everyone has a bad day sometimes. This is helpful information for children learning to regulate their moods. (Ages 4–8)

Wells, R. (1998). *Yoko.* New York: Hyperion Books for Children.
> When Yoko brings a sushi lunch to school, she wonders if her classmates will tease her. Will Yoki feel pressure to give up the lunch she loves to fit into the group? (Ages 4–8)

White, E. B. (1970). *The trumpet of the swan.* New York: HarperCollins.
> E. B. White tells the story of a trumpeter swan who is born without a voice and who must take some unusual risks. It is a story of resilience and persistence. (Ages 7–10)

Wise Brown, M. (1991). *The runaway bunny* (C. Hurd, Illus.). New York: Harper & Row.
> A young bunny who is struggling with separation tries to run away from home to assert his independence, but his mother reminds him that she will always be there to help and to love. (Ages 1½–4)

REFERENCES

Ainsworth, M. D. (1969). Object relations, dependency, and attachment: A theoretical review of the infant-mother relationship. *Child Development, 40,* 969–1025.

Ainsworth, M. D., Belar, M. C., Water, E., & Walls, S. (1978). *Patterns of attachment: A psychological study of the strange situation.* Hillsdale, NJ: Erlbaum.

Anderegg, D. (2003). *Worried all the time: Overparenting in an age of anxiety and how to stop it.* New York: Free Press.

Beck, U., & Willms, J. (2004). *Conversations with Ulrich Beck.* Cambridge, UK: Polity Press.

Beebe, B., & Lachmann, F. M. (1988). Chapter 1: Mother-infant mutual influence and precursors of psychic structure. *Progress in Self Psychology, 3,* 3–25.

Beebe, B., & Sloate, P. (1982). Assesment and treatment of difficulties in mother-infant attunement. *Psychoanalytic Inquiry, 1,* 601–623.

Blegvad, L. (1987). *Anna banana and me* (E. Blegvad, Illus.). New York: Aladdin Publishing Company.

Blos, P. (1967). *On adolescence: A psychoanalytic interpretation.* New York: Free Press.

Bowlby, J. (1982). *Attachment.* New York: Basic Books.

Bowlby, J. (1988). *A secure base.* New York: Basic Books.

Bradshaw, G. A., & Schore, A. N. (2007). How elephants are opening doors: Developmental neuroethology, attachment, and social context. *Ethology, 113,* 426–436.

Brooks, R., & Goldstein, S. (2001). *Raising resilient children.* New York: McGraw-Hill.

Buchanan, A., & Hudson, B. (Eds.). (2000). *Promoting children's emotional well-being.* New York: Oxford.

Bullard, S. (1996). *Teaching tolerance: Rasing open-minded, empathetic children.* New York: Doubleday.

Burton, V. L. (1937). *Choo choo.* New York: Houghton Mifflin.

Calkins-McCormick, L., & Bellino, L. (1997). *Raising lifelong learners: A parent's guide.* Cambridge, MA: Perseus Books.

Cannon, J. (1993). *Stellaluna.* New York: Harcourt Children's Books.

Chess, S., & Thomas, A. (1986). *Temperament in clinical practice.* New York: Guilford Press.

Chess, S., & Thomas, A. (1996). *Temperament: Theory and practice.* New York: Brunner/Mazel.

Cleary, B. (1995). *Ramona the brave* (A. Tiegreen, Illus.). New York: Avon Books. (Original published in 1975)

Cockerham, W. C. (2006). *Society of risk-takers.* New York: Worth Publishers.

Cohen, B. (1983). *Molly's pilgrim* (D. M. Duffy, Illus.).. New York: Lothrop, Lee, & Shephard.

Cohen, J. (Ed.) (1999). *Educating minds and hearts: Social emotional learning and the passage into adolescence.* New York: Teachers College Press.

Coleman, J., & Hagell, A. (Eds.). (2006). *Adolescence, risk, and resilience.* New York: Wiley.

Corkille-Briggs, D. (1970). *Your child's self-esteem: Step-by-step guidelines for raising responsible, productive, happy children.* Garden City, NY: Doubleday.

Dahl, R. (1988). *Matilda* (Q. Blake, Illus.). New York: Penguin Books.

Dalgliesh, A. (1954). *The courage of Sarah Noble* (L. Weisgard, Illus.). New York: Atheneum Books for Young Readers.

Danneberg, J. (2000). *First day jitters* (J. Love, Illus.). Watertown, MA: Charlesbridge.

Dehart, L., Sroufe, A., Cooper, R. (2004). *Child development: Its nature and course.* New York: McGraw-Hill.

Denney, D. (2005). *Risk and society.* London: Sage.

DiCamillo, K. (2006) *The miraculous journey of Edward Tulane* (B. Ibatoulline, Illus.). Cambridge, MA: Candlewick Press.

Doidge, N. (2007). *The brain that changes itself: Stories of personal triumph from the frontiers of brain science.* New York: Penguin.

Douglas, M. (1992). *Risk and blame.* New York, NY: Routledge.

Elkind, D. (1988). *The hurried child: Growing up too fast too soon.* New York: Addison-Wesley.

Eppler-Wolff, N., & Davis, S. (2009). Helping children take good risks. *The Parents League Review* (New York), 122–128.

Erikson, E. H. (1950). *Childhood and society.* New York: W. W. Norton.

Flack, M. (1933). *The story about Ping* (K. Wiese, Illus.). New York: Viking.

Fonagy, P., Gergely, G., Jurist, E. L., & Target, M. (2002). *Affect regulation, mentalization, and the development of the self.* New York: Other Press.

Fonagy, P., & Target, M. (2002). Early intervention, the development of self-regulation. *Psychoanalytic Inquiry, 22,* 307–335.

Fonagy, P., & Target, M. (2005). Bridging the transmission gap: An end to the important mystery of attachment research? *Attachment and Human Development, 7,* 333–343.

Fraser, M. (Ed.). (2004). *Risk and resilience in childhood: An ecological perspective.* Washington, DC: NASW Press.

Fraser, M., Kirby, L. D., & Smokowski, P. R. (2004). Risk and resilience in childhood. In M.W. Fraser (Ed.), *Risk and resilience in childhood* (pp. 13–66). Washington, DC: NASW Press.

Freud, A. (1947). Emotional and instinctual development. In R.W. B. Ellis (Ed.), *Child health and development* (196–215). London: J. & A. Churchill.

Freud, A. (1951). Observations on child development. *The Psychoanalytic Study of the Child, 6,* 18–30.

Freud, A. (1962). Assessment of childhood disturbances. *Psychoanalytic Study of the Child, 17,* 149–158.

Freud, A. (1965). *The writings of Anna Freud: Vol. 4: Normality and pathology in childhood.* New York: International Universities Press.

Freud, A. (1988). The nursery school of the Hampstead child-therapy clinic. *Bulletin of the Anna Freud Centre, 11,* 265–269

Freud, S. (1953). Three essays on theory of sexuality. In J. Strachey (Ed.), *The standard edition of the complete works of Sigmund Freud. Vol. VII.* London: Hogarth Press. (Original work published 1905)

Freud, S. (1963). Introductory lectures on psychoanalysis. Lecture XXII. In J. Strachey (Ed.), *The complete works of Sigmund Freud. Vol. XVI.* London: Hogarth Press. (Original work published 1915–1917)

Freud, S. (1989). The dissolution of the Oedipus complex. In P. Gay (Ed.), *The Freud Reader* (pp. 661–666). New York: W. W. Norton. (Original work published 1924)

Gardner, H. (1983). *Frames of mind: theory of multiple intelligences.* New York: Basic Books.

Gardner, H. (1999). *Intelligence reframed: Multiple intelligences for the 21st century.* New York: Basic Books.

Gardner, H. (2006). *Multiple intelligence: New horizons.* New York: Basic Books.

Gardner, R. A. (1968). The mutual storytelling technique: Use in alleviating childhood oedipal problems. *Contemporary Psychoanalysis, 4,* 161–177.

Gesell, A. L. (1946). *The child from five to ten.* Lanham, MD: Hamilton Press.

Gesell, A. L. (1955). *Child behavior.* New York: Dell.

Gesell, A. L., Ilg, F. L., & Ames, L. B. (1956). *Youth: The years from ten to sixteen.* New York: Harper & Row.

Giddens, A. (1991). *Modernity and self-identity.* Cambridge: Polity Press.

Gilligan, C. (1993). *In a different voice: Psychological theory and women's development.* Cambridge, MA: Harvard University Press.

Ginott, H. G. (1965). *Between parent and child.* New York: Macmillan.

Goleman, D. (1995). *Emotional intelligence: Why it can matter more than IQ.* New York: Bantam.

Goleman, D. (2006). *Social intelligence: The revolutionary new science of human relationships.* New York: Bantam.

Gould, E., & Gross, C. (2002). Neurogenesis in adult mammals: Some progress and problems. *The Journal of Neuroscience, 22,* 619–623.

Greenspan, S., & Salmon, J. (1995). *The challenging child: Understanding, raising, and enjoying the five "difficult" types of children.* Cambridge, MA: Perseus.

Grossman, K. E., Grossman, K., & Waters, E. (2005). *Attachment from infancy to adulthood.* New York: Guilford Press.

Henkes, K. (2006). *Lilly's big day.* New York: Greenwillow Books.

Holt, J., Jr., Stamell, J., & Field, M. (1996). *Celebrate your mistakes: And 77 other risk-taking, out-of-the-box ideas from our best companies.* Burr Ridge, IL: Irwin Professional Publications.

Hyland, D. (1984). *The question of play.* New York: University Press of America.

Isaacs, S. (1966). *Intellectual growth in young children.* New York: Schocken Books.

Kagan, J. (1984). *The nature of the child.* New York: Basic Books.

Kagan, J. (2006). *An argument for mind.* New Haven, CT: Yale University Press.

Kagan, J., & Snidman, N. (2004). *The long shadow of temperament.* Cambridge, MA: Harvard University Press.

Kanfer, R., Ackerman, P. L. & Cudeck. R. (Eds). (1989). *Abilities, motivation, and methodology* (The Minnesota symposium on learning and individual differences). Mahwah, NJ: Erlbaum.

Karen, R. (1998). *Becoming attached.* New York: Oxford University Press.

Klein, M. (1923). The development of a child. *International Journal of Psychoanalysis, 4,* 419–474.

LD OnLine. (1998). Helping the student with ADHD in the classroom: Strategies for teachers. Retrieved June 8, 2008, from http://www.ldonline.org/article/5911

LeDoux, J. (1996). *The emotional brain: The mysterious underpinnings of emotional life.* New York: Simon & Schuster.

Lee, H. (1960). *To kill a mockingbird.* Philadelphia: Lippincott.

Levine, M. (1992). *All kinds of minds.* Cambridge, MA: Educators Publishing.

Levine, M. (2002). *A mind at a time.* New York: Simon & Schuster.

Levine, M. (2005). *Ready or not, here life comes.* New York: Simon & Schuster.

Levine, M. (2006). *The price of privilege: How parental pressure and material advantage are creating a generation of disconnected and unhappy kids.* New York: Harper Collins.

Levine, M., Carey, W., & Crocker, A. (1999). *Developmental-behavioral pediatrics*. Philadelphia: Saunders Publishing.

Levy-Warren, M. H. (1996). *The adolescent journey: Development, identity, formation, and psychotherapy*. Northvale, NJ: J. Aronson.

Linden, D. E. J. (2006, March 7). How psychotherapy changes the brain: The contribution of functional neuro-imaging. *Molecular Psychiatry, 11*, 528–538. Retrieved May 16, 2008, from http://www.nature.com/mp/journal/v11/n6/abs/4001816a.html

Lionni, L. (1963). *Swimmy*. New York: Knopf.

Lowry, L. (1989). *Number the stars*. New York: Bantam Doubleday Dell Books for Young Readers.

Lupton, D. (1999). *Risk*. New York, NY: Routledge.

Lyng, S. (Ed.) (2005). *Edgework: The sociology of risk-taking*. London: Taylor & Francis Group.

Maag, J. W., & Kotlash, J. (1994). Review of stress inoculation training with children and adolescents: Issues and recommendations. *Behavior Modification, 18*(4), 443–469.

Madaras, L., & Madaras, A. (2007). *The "what's happening to my body" book for girls* (3rd ed.). New York: Newmarket Press.

Madaras, L., & Madaras, A. (2009). *The "what's happening to my body" book for boys* (3rd ed.). New York: Newmarket Press.

Mahler, M. S. (1968). *On human symbiosis and the vicissitudes of individuation*. New York: International Universities Press.

Mahler, M. S., Pine, F., & Bergman, A. (1975). *The psychological birth of the human infant. Symbiosis and individuation*. New York: Basic Books.

Martin, B., Jr., & Archambault, J. (1989). *Chicka chicka boom boom* (L. Ehlert, Illus.). New York: Simon & Schuster Books for Young Readers.

Milne, A. A. (1996). *The complete tales of Winnie-the-Pooh* (E. H. Shepard, Illus.). New York: Dutton. (Original work published 1926)

Mogel, W. (2001). *The blessing of a skinned knee. Using Jewish teachings to raise self-reliant children*. New York: Penguin Books.

Moll, J., Kreuger, F., Zahn, R., Pardini, M., de Oliviera-Souza, R., & Grafman, J. (2008). Human fronto-mesolimbic networks guide decisions about charitable donation. *Proceedings of the National Academy of Sciences of the United States of America, 103*(42), 15623–15628.

Naylor, P. R. (1991). *Shiloh* (B. Moser, Illus.). New York: Simon & Schuster.

Newton, C. (1996). *Risk it: Empowering young people to become positive risk takers in the classroom and in life*. Nashville, TN: Incentive Publications.

O'Neil, A. (2002). *The recess queen* (L. Huliska-Beith, Illus.). New York: Scholastic Press.

Piaget, J. (1998). *Jean Piaget: Selected works*. London: Routledge.

Pinkney, B. (1998). *JoJo's flying sidekick*. New York: Aladdin Paperbacks.

Pinkwater, D. M. (1977) *Big orange splot*. New York: Scholastic.

Piper, W. (1930). *The little engine that could* (D. Hauman & G. Hauman, Illus.). New York: Platt and Munk Publishers.

Polacco, P. (1998). *Thank you, Mr. Falker*. New York: Philomel Books.

Potter, B. (1902). *The tale of Peter Rabbit*. London: Frederick Warne.

Schore, A. N. (2002a). Advances in neuropsychoanalysis, attachment theory, and trauma research. *Psychoanlytic Inquiry, 22*, 433–484.

Schore, A. N. (2002b). Dysregulation of the right brain: A fundamental mechanism of traumatic attachment and the psychogenesis of posttraumatic stress disorder. *Australian and New Zealand Journal of Psychiatry, 36*, 9–30.

Schore, A. N. (2005). A neuropsychoanalytic viewpoint: Commentary on paper by Steve Knoblauch. *Psychoanalytic Dialogues, 15*, 829–854.

Schore, A. N., & Schore, J. R. (2008). Modern attachment theory: The central role of affect regulation in development and treatment. *Clinical Social Work Journal, 36*, 9–20.

Sendak, M. (1963). *Where the wild things are*. New York: HarperCollins.

Seuss, Dr. (1960). *Green eggs and ham*. New York: Random House.

Seuss, Dr. (1990). *Oh, the places you will go*. New York: Random House.

Seuss, Dr. (1958). *Yertle the Turtle and other stories*. New York: Random House.

Shandler, S. (1999). *Ophelia speaks: Adolescent girls write about their search for self*. New York: HarperCollins.

Siegel, D. J. (1999). *The developing mind: How relationships and the brain interact to shape who we are*. New York: Guilford Press.

Siegel, D. J., & Hartzell, M. (2003). *Parenting from the inside out: How a deeper self-understanding can help you raise children who thrive*. New York: J. P. Tarcher/Putnam.

Silverstein, S. (1964). *The giving tree*. New York: HarperCollins.

Smith, S. (1998). *Risk and our pedagogical relation to children: On the playground and beyond*. Albany: State University of New York Press.

Solms, M. (1997). Review of the book *Affect regulation and the origin of the self: The neurobiology of emotional development*, ed. by A. N. Schore. *Journal of American Psychoanalytic Association, 45*, 964–969.

Solms, M. (2000). Preliminaries for an integration of psychoanalysis and neuroscience. *Annals of Psychoanalysis, 28*, 179–200.

Sroufe, L.A. (1985). Attachment classification from the perspective of infant-caregiver relationships and infant temperament. *Child Development, 56*, 1–14.

Sroufe, L. A., Egeland, B., Carlson, E., & Collins, W. A. (2005). *The development of the person: The Minnesota study of risk and adaptation from birth to adulthood*. New York: Guilford Press.

Steig, W. (1986). *Brave Irene*. New York: Farrar, Straus, Giroux.

Stern, D. N. (1985). *The interpersonal world of the infant: A view from psychoanalysis and developmental psychology*. New York: Basic Books.

Turecki, S. (1985). *The difficult child*. New York: Bantam Books.

Tullock, J., & Lupton, D. (2003). *Risk and everyday life*. London: Sage.

Vail, P. (1987). *Smart kids with school problems: Things to know and ways to help*. New York: Penguin Books.

Viorst, J. (1987). *Alexander and the terrible, no good, very bad day* (R. Cruz, Illus.). New York: Aladdin PaperBacks.

Watson, J. B. (1914). *Behavior: An introduction to comparative psychology*. New York; Henry Holt and Company.

Wekerle, C., & Wolfe, D. A. (2002). Child maltreatment. In E. J. Mash & R. A. Barkley (Eds.), *Child psychopathology* (pp. 632–686). New York: Guilford Press.

Wells, R. (1998). *Yoko*. New York: Hyperion Books for Children.

Werner, E., & Smith, R. (1992). *Overcoming the odds: High-risk children from birth to adolescence*. Ithaca: Cornell University Press.

White, E. B. (1970). *The trumpet of the swan*. New York: HarperCollins.

Winnicott, D. W. (1953). Transitional objects and transitional phenomena. *International Journal of Psychoanalysis, 34*, 89–97.

Winnicott, D. W. (1958). The capacity to be alone. *International Journal of Psychoanalysis, 39*, 416–420.

Winnicott, D. W. (1975). Metapsychological and clinical aspects of regression within the psycho-analytical set-up. In *Through paediatrics to psycho-analysis* (pp. 278–294). New York: Basic Books.

Wise Brown, M. (1991). *The runaway bunny* (C. Hurd, Illus.). New York: Harper & Row.

Vedartam, S. (2007, May 28). If it feels good to be good, it might be only natural [Electronic version]. *The Washington Post*, p. A01. Retrieved February 10, 2009, from http://www.washingtonpost.com/wp-dyn/content/article/2007/05/27/AR2007052701056.html

Vaillant, G. E. (2008). *Spiritual evolution: A scientific defense of faith*. New York: Broadway.

INDEX

Academic success, 18
Achievement, as emotional risk, 45–46, 110
Ackerman, P. L., 55
Active listening, 76, 83–85
Adolescence
  early, 42
  late, 42–43
  middle, 42
Adolescent Journey, The (Levy-Warren), 168
Affect regulation, 70
  cognitive-emotional maps for, 96–97
  right hemisphere and, 101–102
Ainsworth, Mary D., 97–99
Alcott, Louisa May, 164–165
Alexander and the Terrible, No Good, Very Bad Day (Viorst), 172
All Kinds of Minds (Levine), 56, 168
Ambivalent attachment, 99
Amygdala, temperament and, 87–88
Anderegg, D., 6
Anna Banana and Me (Blegvad), 169
Archambault, J., 171
Attachment
  beyond infancy, 97–101
  cognitive-emotional maps for, 96–97
  during infancy, 96–97
  risk-taking and, 96–101, 102
  types of, 99–100
Attentional abilities, 118
Attunement, 97

Avoidant attachment, 99

Beck, Ulrich, 19–20
Beebe, B., 96, 97–98
Behaviorism, 98
Belar, M. C., 98–99
Bellino, L., 167
Bergman, A., 157, 168–169
Between Parent and Child (Ginott), 168
Big Orange Splot (Pinkwater), 171
Blegvad, L., 169
Blessing of a Skinned Knee, The (Mogel), 169
Block play, 2
Blos, P., 41
Body language, 73
Bowlby, John, 96, 97–98
Bradshaw, G. A., 101
Brain That Changes Itself, The (Doidge), 168
Brave Irene (Steig), 172
Buddy work, Cookies & Dreams program, 133–135
Building games, 162
Bullard, Sara, 132, 167
Burton, V. L., 169

Calkins-McCormick, L., 167
Cannon, J., 169
Carlson, E., 99–100
Cautious child, 115–116
Center for Learning Differences, 56

Challenging Child, The (Greenspan & Salmon), 168
Charles and Tiffany (parent-child pair)
emotional risk-taking and, 19
introduction, 7, 28–29
listening and, 9–10
risk journals and, 31–32
risk-taking and, 90–92
steps toward thoughtful risk-taking, 32–35
storytelling games and, 150–153
Checklists
for listening, 84
for self-reflection, 65, 67, 68–69
Chess, S., 87, 88, 92–93
Chicka Chicka Boom Boom (Martin & Archambault), 171
Child development, 36–60
importance of understanding, 43–44
individual differences in, 38–39
learning style and risk-taking, 55–59, 60, 118–121
life challenges and risk-taking, 59–60
overview, 38–43
risk-taking as part of, 7, 51–55
stages of, 39–43
universal emotional risks, 44–51, 109–114
Childhood and Society (Erikson), 168
Choo Choo (Burton), 169
Cleary, B., 169
Cliques, 129
Cockerham, William C., 21
Cognitive-emotional maps, 96–97
Cohen, B., 170
Cohen, Jonathan, 18, 122, 167
Coleman, J., 37
Collaborative for the Advancement of Social Emotional Learning, 122
Collins, W. A., 99–100
Common Cents, 133
Communication, about learning difficulty/disability, 57
Community service activities, 163–164

Compassion, as learned behavior, 144–145
Competence, upside of risk and, 3–4
Conflict mediation, 133
Connection
cognitive-emotional maps for, 96–97
as emotional risk, 49
Cookies & Dreams program, 133–135
Cooper, R., 97
Corkille-Briggs, D., 167
Courage of Sarah Noble, The (Dalgliesh), 170
Creativity, as emotional risk, 46
Cudeck, R., 55
Cultural components, of risk-taking, 20
cummings, e. e., 61

Dahl, R., 170
Dalai Lama, 127
Dalgliesh, A., 170
Danneberg, J., 170
DeHart, L., 97
Delayed gratification, as emotional risk, 46–48, 110
Denney, D., 15
de Oliviera-Souza, R., 143
Developing Mind, The (Siegel), 169
Developmental tasks. *See* Child development
DiCamillo, K., 170
Difficult Child, The (Turecki), 169
Difficult child (Chess and Thomas), 87
Disappointment, tolerating, 25–26
Distractible child, 117
Divorce, risk-taking and, 59–60
Doidge, N., 88, 104, 168
Doll play, 153–154
Douglas, Mary, 20
Dramatic play, 2, 153–154
Drawing games, 159–161
example of use, 159–161
working with, 160–161

Each Teach program, 133, 135–136
Easy child (Chess and Thomas), 87

Edgeworkers
  nature of, 21
  as risk-takers, 20–22
Educating Minds and Hearts (Cohen), 167
Egeland, B., 99–100
Elkind, D., 6
Emotional Brain, The (LeDoux), 168
Emotional Intelligence (Goleman), 17, 168
Emotional regulation. *See* Affect regulation
Emotional risk, 16–19
  components of, 16–18
  curriculum for developing, 122–126
  listening and letting child feel, 82–83
  nature of, 18–19
  in school, 108–114, 122–126
  types of, 45–51, 110
  universal emotional risks, 44–51, 109–114
Empathy
  attachment and, 100
  goodness of fit and, 93
  listening to build, 76–79
Encountering the unknown (Hyland), 22
Environment
  environmental learning and, 17
  in modifying temperament, 115
Erikson, Eric H., 3–4, 38, 43–44, 50, 168
Ethical Culture School (New York City), 134
Ethics, 11–12

Failure, tolerating, 25–26
Family of origin, self-reflection and, 66–67
Field, M., 109
Fieldston School (Riverdale, New York), 135
First Day Jitters (Danneberg), 170
Fit, parent-child. *See* Goodness of fit (Chess and Thomas)
Flack, M., 170

Fonagy, P., 96, 97–98, 102
Fraser, Mark, 37
Freud, Anna, 38, 51
Freud, Sigmund, 38
Fromm, Erich, 108
Frustration tolerance, of risk-takers, 26

Games, 147–162
  building, 162
  drawing, 159–161
  physical, 157–159
  singing, 161–162
  storytelling, 149–154
  story-writing, 154–157
Gardner, Howard, 56
Gardner, Richard A., 149–150
Gergely, G., 96, 97–98
Gesell, A. L., 38
Giddens, A., 19
Ginott, Haim G., 73, 168
Giving Tree, The (Silverstein), 172
Goethe, J. W. von, 36
Going for it, by risk-takers, 24–25
Goleman, Daniel, 17, 56, 144, 168
Good-enough mothering (Winnicott), 75–76, 97
Goodness of fit (Chess and Thomas), 92–95, 103, 104–105, 107
Gottschalk, Barbara, 136–137
Gould, E., 88
Grafman, J., 143
Green Eggs and Ham (Seuss), 170
Greenspan, Stanley, 88, 168
Gross, C., 88
Grossman, K. E., 100

Hagell, A., 37
Hartzel, M., 169
Henkes, K., 170
Henriques, Mrs., 122–126
High-energy child, 117
Holt, J., Jr., 109
Hyland, D., 15, 22
Hypothalamus, temperament and, 87–88

Illness, risk-taking and, 59–60
Impulsive child, 117
Inattentive child, 117–118
Independence, as emotional risk, 46
Individual differences
   in child development, 38–39
   in risk-taking, 20
   in temperament, 87–92
Industrial Revolution, 19–20
Infancy/toddlerhood stage of develop-
      ment, 39–40
   attachment beyond, 97–101
   attachment during, 96–97
   Strange Situation (Ainsworth et al.),
      98–99
Inflexible child, 117
Inhibited child (Kagan), 87, 88
Insecure attachment, 99, 100
Intellectual development, 38
Intelligences, types of, 56
Interpersonal success, 18
Interpersonal World of the Infant, The
      (Stern), 169
Intimacy, listening to build, 76–79
IQ tests, 17

Jewish Board of Family and Children's
      Services, 135
Jojo's Flying Sidekick (Pinkney), 171
Journals, risk, 31–32
Judy and Hannah (parent-child pair)
   delayed gratification and, 47–48
   goodness of fit and, 94–95
   introduction, 30–31
   learning style and, 119–121
   listening and, 79–80
   self-reflection and, 63–66
   service learning and, 139–143
   story-writing games and, 155–157
Jurist, E. L., 96, 97–98

Kagan, Jerome, 10, 17, 87, 88, 100
Kanfer, R., 55
Karen, R., 98
Katie and Dylan (parent-child pair)
   drawing games and, 159–161
   introduction, 4–5, 27–28

learning difficulty/disability, 57–59
   listening and, 78–79
   risk-taking and peer group, 129–132
   self-reflection and, 70–72
Keller, Helen, 126, 146
Kierkegaard, Soren, 1
Kirby, L. D., 37
Klein, Melanie, 38
Kotlash, J., 26
Kreuger, F., 143

Lachmann, F. M., 96, 97–98
Late primary school/middle school
      stage of development, 41–42
LDOnLine, 90
Learning
   early risk-taking, 111
   emotional risk as foundation of,
      109–114
Learning difficulty/disability, 55–59,
      60
Learning Resource Network at the
      Jewish Board for Family and Chil-
      dren's Services, 56
Learning style, risk-taking and, 55–59,
      60, 118–121
LeDoux, J., 101, 168
Left hemisphere, 144
Levine, M., 55, 168
Levy-Warren, M. H., 41, 168
Lilly's Big Day (Henkes), 170
Linden, D. E. J., 102
Lionni, L., 170–171
Listening, 72–85
   accepting all of child's behaviors ver-
      sus, 80–81
   active, 76, 83–85
   to build intimacy and empathy, 76–79
   checklist for, 84
   importance of, 75–76, 83, 165
   letting child feel and, 82–83
   risk-taking and, 8–10, 83
   ruffling feathers through, 79–80
   understanding problem behaviors
      and, 81–82
Little Engine That Could, The (Piper),
      171

Little Women (Alcott), 164–165
Loss, risk-taking and, 59–60
Louis and Chris (parent-child pair)
  emotional risk in school and, 112–114
  introduction, 29–30
  listening and, 73–75, 81
  parent-child connection and, 105–107
  physical games and, 157–158
Low-energy child, 117–118
Lowry, L., 171
Lupton, D., 20
Lyng, Stephen, 15, 20–22, 44

Maag, J. W., 26
Madaras, A., 41
Madaras, L., 41
Mahler, M. S., 40, 157, 168–169
Mahler, Margaret S., 38
Martin, B., Jr., 171
Mastery, as emotional risk, 45–46
Matilda (Dahl), 170
Mentoring programs, Each Teach, 133,
  135–136
Milne, A. A., 147
Minnesota Studies, 99–100
*Miraculous Journey of Edward Tulane,
  The* (DiCamillo), 170
Mogel, W., 80, 169
Moll, J., 143
Molly's Pilgrim (Cohen), 170

National Institute of Neurological Dis-
  orders and Stroke, 143–144
Naylor, P. R., 171
Neurobiology
  of risk, 17, 101–103, 143–144
  temperament and, 87–88
Newton, C., 109
Number the Stars (Lowry), 171

O'Connor, Sandra Day, 86
Oh! The Places You'll Go (Dr. Seuss),
  12–13, 170
O'Neil, A., 171

Pardini, M., 143
Parent-child connection, 86–107. *See*

also Parent-child pairs
  attachment and, 96–101
  community service and, 163–164
  games in, 147–162
  good-enough mothering (Winnicott),
    75–76, 97
  neurobiology of risk and, 101–103
  parent-child fit and, 92–95, 103,
    104–105, 107
  self-reflection about, 104, 106
  temperament in, 86–92
Parent-child pairs. *See also* Parent-child
  connection
  Charles and Tiffany, 7, 9–10, 19, 28–
    29, 31–35, 90–92, 150–153
  Judy and Hannah, 30–31, 47–48, 63–
    66, 79–80, 94–95, 119–121, 139–143,
    155–157
  Katie and Dylan, 4–5, 27–28, 57–59,
    70–72, 78–79, 129–132, 159–161
  Louis and Chris, 29–30, 73–75, 81,
    105–107, 112–114, 157–158
Parenting From the Inside Out (Siegel &
  Hartzell), 169
Parents
  addressing risk-taking in school,
    123–124
  history of risk and, 22–23
  preparing children for risk-taking,
    6–12
  risky nature of world and, 5–6,
    111–114
  temperament of, 92
Peer groups
  risk-taking and, 128–132
  types of, 129
Physical games, 157–159
  example of use, 157–158
  working with, 158–159
Piaget, Jean, 38
Pine, F., 157, 168–169
Pinkney, B., 171
Pinkwater, D. M., 171
Piper, W., 171
Play, 147–162
  basics of, 148–149
  block, 2

dramatic, 2, 153–154
games to encourage risk-taking,
    147–162
Minnesota Studies and, 99–100
playground and risk society, 22
risk-taking and, 12–13, 147–162
Pleasure, of risk-takers, 26–27
Polacco, P., 171
Potter, B., 171
Poverty, 37
Preschool stage of development, 40,
    52–53
Pride in achievements, of risk-takers,
    26–27
Primary school stage of development,
    40–41, 122–126
  common risks, 53–55
  curriculum for emotional risk-taking,
    122–126
  late, 41–42
Problem behaviors, understanding
    through listening, 81–82
Problem solving, 101
Processing abilities, 118
Project for Social Emotional Learning,
    122
Psychoanalysis, 38
*Psychological Birth of the Human Infant,
    The* (Mahler et al.), 168–169
Psychological development, 38
Psycho-sexual development, 38
Puppet play, 153–154

Questions, for self-reflection, 65–66,
    67–69

Raising Lifelong Learners (Calkins-Mc-
    Cormick & Bellino), 167
Ramona the Brave (Cleary), 169
Recess Queen, The (O'Neil), 171
Reciprocity, 96
Resilience, 37
Right hemisphere, 101–102, 144
Risk. *See also* Risk-taking
  child's response to, 6

downside of, 5, 15–16
emotional. *See* Emotional risk
experiencing uncertainty in, 22
redefining, 2–5
in society. *See* Risk society
upside of, 3–4, 15–16
Risk journals, 31–32
Risk society, 19–23
  becoming a risk society, 19–20
  defined, 20
  edgeworkers as risk-takers, 20–22
  history of risk and parents, 22–23
  individual differences in risk-taking,
    20
  playground, 22
Risk-taking. *See also* Risk
  attachment and, 96–101, 102
  breaking barriers and, 132–137
  characteristics of good risk-taker,
    23–27
  components of, 16–18
  connection with temperament, 10–11,
    86–92, 102, 114–118
  defined, 15–19
  edgeworkers as risk-takers, 20–22
  encouraging/tempering, 24–25
  essential place in raising children, 2
  games to encourage, 147–162
  guidelines for creating positive risk-
    taking programs, 140–141
  individual differences in, 20
  learning style and, 55–59, 60, 118–121
  life challenges and, 59–60
  listening to encourage, 8–10, 83
  neurobiology of, 17, 101–103, 143–144
  parent-child fit and, 92–95, 103,
    104–105, 107
  as part of development, 7, 51–55
  peer groups and, 128–132
  play and, 12–13, 147–162
  preparing children for, 6–12
  risky nature of world and, 5–6,
    111–114
  in school, 11, 18, 108–126
  self-reflection and, 7–8, 104

steps toward thoughtful, 32–35
styles of, 17, 59–60
temperament and, 10–11, 86–92, 102,
  114–118
tolerance and, 11–12
Roosevelt, Eleanor, 14
Runaway Bunny, The (Wise Brown), 172

Salmon, J., 88, 168
School
  curriculum for developing risk-tak-
    ing, 121–126
  emotional risk in, 108–114, 122–126
  foundation of learning and, 109–114
  "Hanging with Dave" activity,
    108–109
  learning style and, 118–121
  risk-taking in, 11, 18, 108–126
  stages of childhood development
    and, 40–43, 52–55
  temperament and, 114–118
Schore, Alan N., 101–102
Schore, J. R., 101–102
Secure attachment, 99, 100
Seeds of Peace program, 133, 136–137
Self-confidence
  listening and, 75–76
  upside of risk and, 3–4, 12–13, 127–
    128, 129
Self-esteem, 18
  listening and, 75–76
Self-expression, as emotional risk,
  49–50, 110
Self-reflection
  advanced topics, 67–72
  checklists for, 65, 67, 68–69
  on curriculum for emotional risk-
    taking in school, 126
  discovering family of origin, 66–67
  about learning difficulty/disability,
    57
  about parent-child connection, 104,
    106
  by parents, 62–72
  questions for, 65–66, 67–69

risk-taking and, 7–8, 104
ruffling feathers through, 63–65
Self-respect, risk-taking and, 127–128
Sendak, M., 171
Separation, as emotional risk, 46, 99,
  110
Service learning programs, 137–143
Seuss, Dr., 12–13, 170
Shared storytelling. *See* Storytelling
  games
Shiloh (Naylor), 171
Shy, cautious child, 115–116
Siegel, D. J., 169
Silence, 77–78
Silverstein, S., 172
Singing games, 161–162
Sloate, P., 96
Slow-to-warm-up child (Chess and
  Thomas), 87, 88
Smith, R., 37
Smith, S., 15, 22
Smokowski, P. R., 37
Snidman, N., 17, 87, 100
Social-emotional learning, 18, 101–103
Social intelligence, 17
Society. *See* Risk society
Solms, M., 101
Soothing, goodness of fit and, 93
Spiritual Evolution (Vaillant), 144
Spock, Benjamin, 63
Spoiling a child, 98
Sroufe, L. Alan, 97–100
Stages of childhood development,
  39–43
  early adolescence (13 to 15), 42
  infancy/toddlerhood (birth to 3s),
    39–40, 96–97, 98–99
  late adolescence (18+), 42–43
  late primary school/middle school
    (10 to 13), 41–42
  middle adolescence (15 to 17), 42
  preschool (3 to 5), 40, 52–53
  primary school (5 to 10), 40–41,
    53–55, 122–126
  risk-taking and, 111

Stamell, J., 109
Steig, W., 172
Stellaluna (Cannon), 169
Stern, D. N., 40, 96, 98, 169
Story about Ping, The (Flack), 170
Storytelling games, 149–154
   aspects of shared storytelling, 149–150
   example of use, 150–153
   with older children, 153–154
   working with, 152–153
Story-writing games, 154–157
   example of use, 155–157
   working with, 157
Strange Situation (Ainsworth et al.), 98–99
Styles
   learning, 55–59, 60, 118–121
   of risk-taking, 17, 59–60
Success, types of, 18
Summer camp program, Seeds of Peace, 133, 136–137
Swimmy (Lionni), 170–171

Tale of Peter Rabbit, The (Potter), 171
Target, M., 96, 97–98, 102
Teachers
   curriculum for emotional risk-taking, 122–126
   learning difficulty/disability and, 56
Teaching Tolerance (Bullard), 132, 167
Temperament
   biological basis of, 87–88
   connection with risk-taking, 10–11, 86–92, 102, 114–118
   fluidity of, 17
   goodness of fit and, 107
   impulsive, distractible, high-energy child, 117
   individual differences in, 87–92
   inflexible child, 117
   innate, 87
   low-energy, inattentive child, 117–118
   nature of, 86–87
   of parents, 92

risk-taking and, 10–11, 86–92, 102, 114–118
   shy, cautious child, 115–116
   types of, 87
Tenacity, of risk-takers, 26
Tenderness, 98
Thank You, Mr. Falker (Polacco), 171
Thomas, A., 87, 88, 92–93
Tolerance
   compassion as learned behavior, 144–145
   Cookies & Dreams program, 133–135
   Each Teach program, 133, 135–136
   guidelines for creating positive risk-taking programs, 140–141
   nature of, 132–133
   risk-taking and, 11–12
   scientific explanation for taking risk to care, 143–144
   Seeds of Peace program, 133, 136–137
   service learning programs, 137–143
   teaching, 133–137
Trumpet of the Swan, The (White), 172
Trust, as emotional risk, 50
Tullock, J., 20
Turecki, Stanley, 88, 169
Tutoring programs, Each Teach, 133, 135–136

Uncertainty, as emotional risk, 50–51, 110

Vail, P., 55
Vaillant, George E., 144
Vedartam, S., 143–144
Viorst, J., 172
Volunteer activities, 163–164

Waiting, as emotional risk, 46–48
Wallach, John, 136
Walls, S., 98–99
Waters, E., 98–99, 100
Watson, John B., 98
Wekerle, C., 66
Wells, R., 172

Werner, E., 37
Where the Wild Things Are (Sendak), 171
White, E. B., 172
Willms, J., 20
Winnicott, D. W., 46, 75–76, 97
Wise Brown, M., 172
Wolfe, D. A., 66
Work, risk-taking and, 12–13
Writing
  in risk journals, 31–32
  in story-writing games, 154–157

Yertle the Turtle and Other Stories
    (Seuss), 170
Yoko (Wells), 172
Your Child's Self-Esteem (Corkille-
    Briggs), 167

Zahn, R., 143

ABOUT THE AUTHORS

Susan Davis, Ph.D., is a clinical psychologist in private practice in Manhattan. She is also a staff psychologist and assistant professor at Montefiore Medical Center of the Albert Einstein College of Medicine, and a consultant to the Saul and Carole Zabar Nursery School at the Jewish Community Center in Manhattan.

Nancy Eppler-Wolff, Ph.D., is a clinical psychologist and psychoanalyst in private practice in Manhattan. She is also an honorary adjunct assistant professor and clinical supervisor at Teachers College, Columbia University, and an adjunct assistant professor and clinical supervisor at the Derner Institute at Adelphi University.